Pu-erh Tea

Appreciating Chinese Tea

Written by Wang Jidong
Translated by Chen Zhufen and Liu Qingling

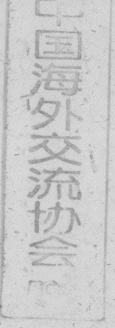

CHINA INTERCONTINENTAL PRESS

WORLD CULTURE BOOKS

图书在版编目（CIP）数据

普洱茶：英文/王缉东著；陈铸芬，刘清伶译.
-北京：五洲传播出版社，2009.12
ISBN 978-7-5085-1743-8

Ⅰ.①普… Ⅱ.①王… ②陈… ③刘… Ⅲ.①茶-文化-云南省-英文 Ⅳ.①TS971

中国版本图书馆CIP数据核字（2009）第216778号

Original Chinese language edition copyright © 2009 by China Light Industry Press

著　　者：王缉东
译　　者：陈铸芬　刘清伶
选题编辑：荆孝敏　世界文化图书
责任编辑：王　莉 Lisa Zhang
装帧设计：宋索迪
设计制作：世界文化图书

出版发行：五洲传播出版社
地　　址：北京市海淀区北小马厂6号华天大厦
邮　　编：100038
网　　址：www.cicc.org.cn
电　　话：010-58891281
印　　刷：恒美印务（广州）有限公司
开　　本：889×1194mm　1 / 32
印　　张：5
版　　次：2010年1月第1版 2010年1月第1次印刷
07980（平）

Contents

Thanks to Jing Xiaomin, Li Mei, Madhumita Bardhan Sinha, Wang Li, Lisa Zhang and Suodi Song for their tireless efforts to make the project possible.

A Visit to the Ancient Tea Trees in the Remote Mountains

Ancient tea trees more than 800 years old in Nannuo Mountain

You have to visit the virgin forests in southwest Yunnan to see the original ancient tea trees. Oblivious to the changing market economy, these trees remain unmoved, watching the mountain fog gathering and clearing all year round. Unlike young trees which flourish every season padding the tea farmers' wallets, ancient trees slow down their growth, showing dignity. The phrase "tea from wild ancient trees" touches your heart, transporting you to the vast fields and remote mountains, offering tranquility.

King of tea trees in Nannuo Mountain

Young 20–30-year-old tea trees at the foot of ancien 400–500-year-old tea tree

Leaves of ancient tea trees in Yiwu

Leaves of ancient tea trees in Yibang

"Crab pincers" of ancient arbor tea trees in Nannuo Mountain

Blossoms of the ancient tea trees in Gaoshan Village of Yiwu

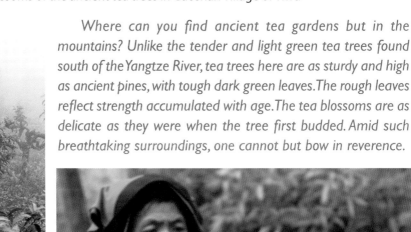

Where can you find ancient tea gardens but in the mountains? Unlike the tender and light green tea trees found south of the Yangtze River, tea trees here are as sturdy and high as ancient pines, with tough dark green leaves. The rough leaves reflect strength accumulated with age. The tea blossoms are as delicate as they were when the tree first budded. Amid such breathtaking surroundings, one cannot but bow in reverence.

A Hani tea farmer of Bangzha Community in Pu-erh

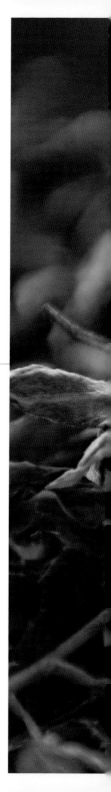

Part 1

Learning about Pu-erh Tea from Its Processing Techniques

The increasing popularity of Pu-erh tea arouses people's interest in it. To know Pu-erh tea, you must first learn about its processing techniques. Many mysteries are rooted in its processing procedures. Learning about them and their techniques will help unveil the mysteries.

I. Chinese Tea Classifications and Pu-erh Tea

Pu-erh tea is not just dark tea but the most famous type of dark tea today.

(I) Classifications of Chinese Tea

China produces various kinds of tea. According to incomplete statistics, China has over 1,000 varieties of famous teas. Tea is classified according to different standards, including processing technique, place of origin, production season, quality grade, shape and sales.

Classification methods of Chinese tea:

Processing technique:	Green tea, black tea, cyan tea, yellow tea, white tea, dark tea, etc.
Place of origin:	Zhejiang tea, Fujian tea, Taiwan tea, Yunnan tea, Jiangxi tea, Anhui tea, etc.
Production season:	Spring tea (picked before April 19–21, or April 4–5, according to the Chinese calendar), Summer tea, Shu tea (picked from August 7–9 to August 23–24 according to the Chinese calendar), Autumn tea, Winter tea, etc.
Quality grade:	Superfine, first grade, second grade, third grade, fourth grade, fifth grade, etc.
Shape:	Needle-shaped, spiral-shaped, chip-shaped, orchid-shaped, bar-shaped, etc.
Sales:	Export, domestic sales, boundary sales, overseas, etc.
Processing:	Unprocessed, processed, instant black tea, etc.
Fermentation:	Non-fermented, slightly fermented, half-fermented, completely fermented, etc.

 TIPS In modern tea studies, tea is classified into basic tea and reprocessed tea. Basic tea includes green tea, black tea, cyan tea, yellow tea, white tea and dark tea. Reprocessed tea includes jasmine tea, compressed tea, teabag, instant tea, tea drink, etc.

The most commonly used classification of tea:

Tea — Types of basic tea

Green tea

Non-fermented tea (Long Jing tea, Bi Luo Chun, etc.) with green leaves and clear tea liquid. Tender sprouts are used.

White tea

Slightly fermented tea (Baimudan, etc.) with apricot yellow tea liquid.

Yellow tea

Slightly fermented tea (Junshanyinzhen, etc.) with yellow leaves and tea liquid.

Cyan tea

Half-fermented tea (Tieguanyin, Dahongpao, etc.) with golden to orange-red tea liquid, the fragrance of green tea and the mellowness of black tea.

Black tea

Completely fermented tea (Yunnan Dianhong black tea, Qihong Keemun Black Tea, Lapsang Souchong Black Tea, etc.) with sweet red tea liquor and red brewed leaf. Dry tea is dark red or even black.

Dark tea

Post-fermented tea (Pu-erh tea, etc.) with orange or reddish-brown tea liquid and black or brown green tea leaves.

Types of reprocessed tea

Jasmine tea, compressed tea, teabag, instant tea, tea drink, etc.

Pu-erh tea is a type of dark tea. People know very little about dark tea, and the popularity of Pu-erh tea has further obscured the concept "dark tea."

(II) Dark Tea—Pu-erh Tea

Besides Pu-erh tea, there are other types of dark tea which are well-known.

Dark tea is mainly produced in Yunnan, Guangxi, Sichuan, Hubei, Hunan, etc.

1. Dark tea from Hunan

Hunan produces Xiangjian tea, Qianliang tea, Fu brick (Fuzhuan), Black brick (Heizhuan), Flowery brick (Huazhuan), etc. Fu brick is characterized by its growth of fungus spores, which gives it a unique fragrance.

▲ Hunan Qianliang tea

▲ Inside of the Fuzhuan tea with fungus spores

▲ Hunan Qianliang tea packed

▲ Packaged Fuzhuan tea

2. Dark tea from Sichuan

Dark tea from Sichuan is classified into south-road brick tea and west-road brick tea. Samples include Kangzhuan, Jinjian, etc.

▲ Dark tea from Sichuan

▲ Jinjian tea

3. Dark tea from Guangxi

Originally produced in the Liubao township in Cangwu County, it is dark brown and glossy. The tea liquid is dark red and sweet with a betel nut fragrance and a sweet aftertaste. The tea is characterized by its red color, strength, mellowness and age. The best Liubao tea that is old is the one with golden fungus spores. This once commanded the largest market share of dark tea in Hong Kong and the Southeast Asian countries.

▲ Dark colored Liubao tea

▲ Liubao tea

4. Dark tea from Yunnan

The representative Yunnan dark tea is Pu-erh tea. It is produced after a long period of artificial fermentation (in piles with controlled temperature and humidity, details on page 31) of loose Yunnan green tea (Yunnan sun-baked green crude tea). It is usually made into compressed tea, such as the Qizibing (Seven Cakes) tea, brick tea, bowl tea, etc.

Pu-erh tea, very popular in the tea market today, is a representative dark tea—one of the six basic types of tea. It is also the favorite among the types of dark tea. Growing in a pure environment, it is effective in improving digestion and controlling cholesterol and blood pressure. This has increased its function to meet the spiritual and physical need of the modern generation. Its tough transportation route closely associates Pu-erh tea with the ancient tea route.

▲ Pu-erh tea made of fine and tender leaves

▲ Guhua tea

▲ Packaged Qizibing tea

▲ Arbor tea

II. Unveiling the Mysteries of Pu-erh Tea

Why does dark tea (and some types of Oolong tea and black tea) become more fragrant as it gets older? Why does it endure long years of preservation, while other types of tea lose all original color, fragrance and taste?

The primary reason lies in the different raw materials. Tea trees with large leaves contain more substances in their fresh leaves. That is why Pu-erh tea not only endures preservation over longer periods, but also gets mellower and sweeter. After storing for a long time, its tea properties become weak and it has a unique flavor and taste. It transforms from the original astringent taste to become mellow and sweet, and then back to a light taste. While other tea are best when fresh, Pu-erh tea gets better with age. Another reason for Pu-erh's unique taste is its post-fermentation technique.

In the 1990s, the popularity of Pu-erh tea started in Hong Kong and Taiwan and then spread throughout China. The craze for Pu-erh tea is still on the increase, which may well lead to its global popularity. To understand Pu-erh tea, we should learn its production techniques first for many of its mysteries lie in its production process.

(I) What Is Pu-erh Tea?

1. Pu-erh tea: A common man's perspective

Ten years ago, most Chinese outside Yunnan had probably only heard of Pu-erh tea but not seen it. It is only recently that people have started to learn more. Today, drinking Pu-erh tea has become a trend.

The most commonly used terms associated with Pu-erh tea are "raw cake," "processed cake," "mellower with age" and "collection and appreciation." Most drinkers know that Pu-erh tea is a combination of raw tea and processed tea. The uniqueness of Pu-erh tea lies in its becoming "more fragrant with age," a common characteristic of dark teas in general, contrary to the general belief that tea is better when it is fresh.

What is raw tea? What is processed tea? Do both become more fragrant with age? Does Pu-erh tea really become better with age? The answer is not simple. Therein lies the chief attraction of Pu-erh tea—the more you search for the truth, the more elusive it becomes.

2. Pu-erh tea: An expert's perspective

According to tea experts Pu-erh tea is the generic name given to the loose tea and the compressed tea, which conform to the local standards of Yunnan Province. They are sun-baked big-leaf green crude tea processed through fermentation (including natural fermentation and artificial post-fermentation).

Experts specify key points, such as place of origin, type of raw material, processing technique, standard for and form of the final product.

Place of origin: The area under the ancient Pu-erh Prefecture

▲ The ancient town of Pu-erh Prefecture 100 years ago (provided by the Publicity Department of Ninger County)

In 1729, Emperor Yongzheng established the Pu-erh Prefecture. Its administration bureau was in the present Ning'er County. The Pu-erh Prefecture covered the present Pu-erh city (originally Simao City, renamed in April 2007), Xishuangbanna Prefecture and part of Lincang Prefecture. The fresh leaves of the big-leaf tea trees in this area are the first criterion for recognizing Pu-erh tea.

Type of tree and raw material: Sun-baked green crude tea of the big-leaf type

These trees are found only in Yunnan. They have evolved from growing wild to planned planting today. Usually, the leaves are 12–24cm long and their texture is leatherlike—thicker and tougher than leaves of other types of tea trees. Tea trees across the globe have, through continual migration, evolved from the wild big-leaf tea trees. The type of trees used as raw material is an important factor for long-term storage of the tea product.

Pick fresh leaves of the big-leaf tea trees, (usually one sprout and three leaves), stir them in a wok over fire to get rid of the fresh-leaf smell, destroy their enzyme activity, evaporate the moisture and release the fragrance. Twist them into striations and keep out in the sun to turn them into sun-baked green crude tea. This material is used to produce Pu-erh tea.

Techniques: Natural fermentation or artificial fermentation of the sun-baked crude green tea

Compress the sun-baked green crude tea into cakes or bricks. This is known as raw tea. After a specific period of time (5–10, or 10–20 years), under normal temperature and humidity, the raw tea becomes naturally fermented Pu-erh tea.

This technique is called "natural fermentation." Put the sun-baked

▲ Pu-erh tea under natural fermentation

green crude tea (loose tea) in a controlled environment having the appropriate temperature and humidity conducive to its fermentation and help it ferment quickly, in a process called "Wodui" (pile fermentation). After approximately 40 days, it becomes processed tea. In this book, the term Pu-erh tea refers to the fermented tea which is naturally or artificially fermented—the "processed tea."

◄ Pu-erh tea under artificial pile fermentation

Physicochemical and sensory indices: Conforming to the local standards of Pu-erh tea in Yunnan Province

Post 1973, after repeated testing, the artificial pile fermentation technique has greatly developed. Now there is a distinction between "raw tea" (traditional Pu-erh tea) and "processed tea," which makes the concept of Pu-erh tea more pluralistic. Meanwhile, the industrial standards of artificial fermentation and other related local standards have also been established. The purpose of the artificial pile is to speed up the fermentation of Pu-erh tea.

Artificial fermentation shortens the natural fermentation process of 10 to 20 years to merely days, thereby meeting the needs of the customers.

Thus, Pu-erh tea is the kind of tea whose physicochemical and sensory indices conform to the local standards of Pu-erh tea in Yunnan Province.

▲ Evaluation of Pu-erh tea

Shape of final product: Loose tea or compressed tea

Pu-erh tea can be in the form of fermented loose tea and fermented compressed tea (details on P36).

Tea that can reach the above standards is Yunnan Pu-erh tea.

▲ Loose Pu-erh tea

▲ Compressed Pu-erh tea in the shape of melon

3. Pu-erh tea in the market

It is common knowledge that Pu-erh tea includes raw tea and processed tea, but people usually know little about which type of tea should be stored and for how long. The tea industry defines Pu-erh tea as processed tea.

Among the kinds of Pu-erh tea in the market and those favored by customers, there are Pu-erh tea acknowledged by experts (processed tea only) and the commonly known raw tea. In addition, there is the "several-year-old tea" that falls in-between the raw tea and the processed tea (those that are yet to finish their natural fermentation). Other kinds of tea are those that are preserved for some time after artificial fermentation and the 20–30-year-old tea.

Now let's discuss and learn about Pu-erh tea as a kind of tea offered on the market.

(II) The Processing Technique of Pu-erh Tea

The processing is key to the special fragrance of Pu-erh tea. It is also the source of the various names used to refer to the tea. As artificial fermentation and natural fermentation are two techniques of the later stage of tea processing, let us first divide the tea processing into two stages—the preliminary sun-baking and the later fermentation.

1. Making raw material of Pu-erh tea—sun-baked tea leaves

Picking tea

▲ Picking fresh leaves from the big-leaf tea trees

Whether raw or processed, Pu-erh tea is rich in taste. Unlike green tea, yellow tea or white tea, where farmers need to choose the most tender sprouts, when picking fresh leaves for Pu-erh tea, farmers just pick sprouts with three leaves and some old leaves for their mellow fragrance.

The Pu-erh tea leaves are picked in spring, summer and autumn, but those picked in spring are the best. According to the tea farmers, the fresh leaves and sprouts are picked in batches. In spring they usually pick one or two batches called the first and second batch respectively.

The first image that appears in our mind when visualizing tea-leaf picking is of women deftly picking leaves from the waist-high trees south of Yangtze River. The picking of leaves from the Yunnan big-leaf tea trees are more colorful. This is because the Pu-erh tea grows in regions dominated by the ethnic minorities. During the tea-picking season, the Hani, Blang and Dai people in brightly colored ethnic costumes and accessories paint a pretty picture. Secondly, tea trees in this region are not only large areas of short trees planted in the past 20 to 30 years (the so called terrace tea trees about waist or breast

A Dai woman picking fresh leaves from ancient tea trees

Upper right: Sprouts of 20- to 30-year-old terrace tea trees ◀

Middle right: Autumn tea leaves of ancient tea trees ▶

400- to 500-year-old ancient tea trees in the huge ancient tea garden in Jingmai

height), but also many tall 200-, 300-, 500- and even 800-year-old trees, forming a wonderful landscape.

Pu-erh tea farmers pick the leaves in many ways—simply reaching out their hands, standing on their toes and there are times when they have to climb the trees. The scenes are varied and rarely seen elsewhere.

Withering tea

Withering (or airing) is to reduce the humidity of the fresh leaves, to lower the temperature for baking the leaves and to soften the leaves. The natural process of withering is by exposing leaves to the air, withering in weak sunlight and withering with hot air in the rainy season.

▲ Natural withering by exposing leaves to the air

Sha Qing (heating tea)

Sha Qing is a terminology in processing tea, which means heating and stirring.

Chao Qing, that is steaming, *Zheng Qing* or scalding in boiling water, *Lao Qing* or destroying the enzyme activity, thereby preventing the phenol substances from oxidizing and the fresh leaves from

▲ Heating and stirring big-leaf tea in a wok

turning yellow or red and the quality of tea from changing. Heating keeps the leaves in the desired state. Except for a few types of tea, the first step of processing after picking tea is heating it. Among the many ways, heating in woks, as in Pu-erh tea is most widely used.

Put the fresh leaves in a heated iron wok. Using both hands pick up the tea leaves from the bottom of the wok and scatter them back into the wok. Repeat the process until the leaves are no longer stiff, their color has turned yellowish and you can smell the smoky fragrance of the green leaves.

Airing tea

Transfer the hot leaves into the bamboo basket. Scatter them with care to dispel the heat and cool them quickly to prevent the leaves from further changing due to the heat for the next step of processing.

Rubbing and twisting tea

Rubbing and twisting is to shape the tea leaves for the final product.

If the tea leaf is rubbed and twisted it will take a spiral form, like the green tea Bi Luo Chun.

▲ Scattering and airing

▲ Rubbing and twisting

▲ Distinct striations of aired raw tea leaves

Twist the Pu-erh tea into striations along the stem. Roll the leaves with both hands into a ball, then rub and squeeze them repeatedly forming an oval (like practicing Taiji). Apply pressure evenly. If the pressure is too light, the leaves are unlikely to form striations and there will be no tea extract.

This is not conducive for fermentation. Rubbing or twisting too hard will cause the leaves to break and become unmarketable. Once the tea extract starts oozing out, the hands feel sticky, smell freshly fragrant and turn light green. Stop when the 3 or 4 leaves on the stem have twisted into striations.

Drying tea

The twisted tea leaves are spread in bamboo baskets and put out in the sun to absorb sunlight. These sun-baked green crude tea leaves are the raw material for compressed Pu-erh tea. However, most of the tea-picking time in Yunnan coincides with the rainy season characterized by heavy and continuous rainfall. On rainy days, twisted tea striations are often dried over gentle fire. That is why raw tea leaves picked in the rainy season smell smoky. Today, large quantities of raw tea leaves are machine-dried, yet the traditional sun-baked green crude tea leaves are the best in terms of quality.

▲ Sun-baking

2. Producing naturally fermented Pu-erh tea

Compressing and shaping

Compressing the tea into different shapes eases packaging and transportation over long distances and time. The compressing technology was introduced during the period of the Ming Dynasty. The people of Yunnan reformed the various steps for tea production. Compressing tea by hand is still prevalent in the regions producing traditional Pu-erh tea (e.g., Yiwu).

Tea cakes are traditionally, sun-baked green crude tea leaves compressed into different shapes in the following steps:

1. Weighing: Usually a tea cake weighs 357–400g. Take a suitable amount of tea leaves in a perforated metal steamer.

2. Placing the flyleaf: Position the flyleaf with some striated tea leaves on it.

3. Steaming: Put the metal steamer over the steam to soften and moisturize the tea leaves for convenient compressing and post-fermentation of the tea.

4. Putting in the bag: Overturn the steamer into the cotton bag, and knead the leaves into a pile in the bag.

5. Kneading: Roll the bag tightly, knead the hot tea pile into a tea cake of even thickness, winding the bag into a spiral on top of the cake as shown. Press the spiral-shaped knot into the middle part on the back of the tea cake.

6. Compressing: Put the tea cakes under the special stone and stand on the stone to compress the tea leaves evenly. Today, machines are used to compress the tea leaves, but pressing manually shapes the cakes evenly and neatly.

7. Drying: Take the tea cakes out of the bags to dry in a cool place.

8. Packaging: Pack the tea cakes in cotton paper and fold the edge of the paper into the hole made by the bag knot on the back of the cake.

 TIPS Besides cakes, Pu-erh tea is also compressed into the shape of melons, bricks, mushrooms, etc.

9. Packaging Qizibing tea together: Put seven packaged tea cakes in a pile. Wrap it with sheets made of bamboo shoot skin, bundle it up tightly and then put it in a flat bamboo basket. Bamboo threads are best for tying the cakes because iron wires rust easily and chemical substances in the plastic pollute the tea leaves. Pu-erh tea is often called seven-cake tea.

Long-term storage and natural post-fermentation

After packaging the seven-cake tea you have two options: You can store the tea for a period of time. You can do this by keeping it in a storehouse or just let it ferment naturally (without putting in the storehouse), before selling it according to the market demand. Another way is to directly sell the raw Pu-erh tea.

In the past, large batches of Pu-erh tea were transported to Tibet and other places. Yunnan's and Tibet's rugged terrain made transportation difficult. The combination of the demand for Pu-erh tea, the hazardous route and the lack of roads and proper vehicles led to the world-famous ancient caravan route and the caravan career. The tea matured continuously along the way. Factors such as long exposure to the sun, wind, rain and humidity, the bamboo shoot skin wrap, the wild grass and flowers along the way and the temperature of the horse on which it was laden affected the raw tea cakes, imbuing it with a special fragrance of the Yunnan wilderness. Transportation by ships, too, took a long time, affecting the quality of the tea. That is why Pu-erh tea fermented in natural conditions is especially fragrant and mellow.

Pu-erh tea gained popularity during the middle and late period of the Qing Dynasty. It was the tribute tea to the imperial court during the reign of emperors Yongzheng and Guangxu. However, after the Qing Dynasty, the importance of Pu-erh tea quickly declined and went into oblivion. Today, Pu-erh tea has risen to the fore as a new drink in Taiwan and Hong Kong. Its long-term storage capability has made it regain popularity overnight, and there is great demand for its mellow fragrance and taste.

The present generation's fast pace of living makes time invaluable. There is a sharp gap between the prices of the naturally fermented Pu-erh tea and artificially fermented tea—the more technology develops, the more precious the time-honored natural products become.

3. Producing Pu-erh tea through artificial fermentation

Sorting into piles

Sort the sun-baked green crude tea leaves into different piles according to their quality for pile fermentation.

Pile fermentation

"Pile" means to add moisture to the tea and control its humidity and temperature. In pile fermentation, pile tons of raw tea leaves together, add water, keeping the temperature within 58–60°. The tea leaves are kept thus for 48 days. Fermentation occurs under suitable temperature, humidity and by the chemical reaction of the microbes and enzymes in the leaves.

The leaves turn reddish-brown and the tea liquid is red, bright, thick, mellow and smooth. Pile fermentation is a major step in the production of processed Pu-erh tea. The humidity, temperature, pile-stirring times and degree of fermentation should be flexible; it should be controlled according to the season and the tenderness of the raw tea leaves. Improper fermentation will produce substandard tea. This is why great importance is attached to the origin of the Pu-erh tea. Processed Pu-erh tea of different origin possess different taste and flavor.

Tests show that Pu-erh tea processed through artificial pile fermentation have the same physicochemical indices as the tea through natural fermentation. Post fermentation, the quality of the tea leaves become more stable. Consumers can drink processed tea

▲ Pile fermentation

immediately after buying, or store it for a while to reduce the dryness of the newly processed tea, thereby improving the taste. But there is no need to store it long. The artificially fermented tea is processed to satisfy the market demand ahead of time.

The terms "raw cake," "processed cake," "traditional Pu-erh tea," experts' definition of Pu-erh tea, the industry standards and the terms for techniques and processing are all closely associated with the development of the artificial pile fermentation.

Drying

After pile fermentation, the tea is dried and becomes loose Pu-erh tea.

Selection

After selection by machine comes selection by hand. This step is an important factor to the quality of the tea. Given that machines fail to pick the stem and impurities out from the leaves, only manual selection can guarantee tea quality.

▲ Manual selection

▲ Stems picked out

Moisturizing

Moisturizing is an important step in making processed tea. Before compressing the processed tea, moisture should be added to the dried tea to soften it. After pile fermentation, tea cannot be steamed but can be moisturized to ensure that tea leaves form tight striations and will not crumble during compressing.

▲ Selected tea leaves

Compressing into shapes

The processed loose Pu-erh tea is compressed into different shapes but mostly into cakes.

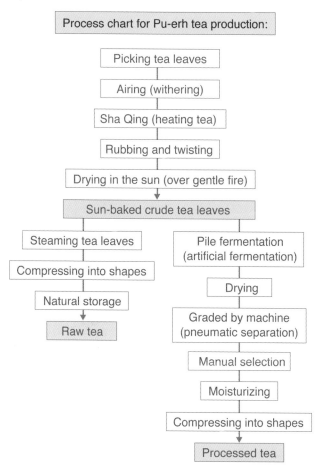

Process chart for Pu-erh tea production:

Picking tea leaves

Airing (withering)

Sha Qing (heating tea)

Rubbing and twisting

Drying in the sun (over gentle fire)

Sun-baked crude tea leaves

Steaming tea leaves

Compressing into shapes

Natural storage

Raw tea

Pile fermentation (artificial fermentation)

Drying

Graded by machine (pneumatic separation)

Manual selection

Moisturizing

Compressing into shapes

Processed tea

We can see that making sun-baked green crude tea leaves remains the same for naturally fermented and manually fermented tea. The difference is in the post-fermentation. The key to natural fermentation is its timing and storage. Artificial fermentation relies on the technology of pile fermentation. There are many factors that affect the quality of Pu-erh tea, which we will analyze one by one after understanding the primary factor—technique.

Part 2

Classification of Pu-erh Tea

Differences give rise to classifications. Pu-erh tea can be classified according to many different guiding principles, among which the following principles are the most popular and closely related to the tea drinkers.

▲ Raw Pu-erh tea cake

◄ Processed Pu-erh tea cake

I. Popular Classification of Pu-erh Tea

1. According to the processing technique: Raw tea and processed tea

Raw tea

As mentioned before, raw tea refers to the sun-baked green crude tea (loose tea) that is made from the fresh tea leaves of the Yunnan big-leaf trees that are heated, twisted and aired before compressing into different shapes.

It is known as crude tea for its simple processing. It is also called Yunnan raw tea for its place of origin. Raw Pu-erh tea is much stronger in taste and property than other types of tea trees.

Raw Pu-erh tea from good raw material, naturally fermented under correct temperature and humidity for 5–10 years or even 20–30 years, is best. The strong tea is softened and its taste becomes mellow.

Tea lovers derive genuine spiritual enjoyment from tasting this tea.

▲ Raw tea cake   ▲ Raw tea liquid

The dry raw tea is dark green in color. The tea liquid is yellowish-green and a little astringent in taste. This may cause a new drinker's tongue and throat to tighten and some digestive discomfort.

Processed Tea

Raw tea turns into processed tea either through natural fermentation over time or pile fermentation (artificial fermentation), which takes much less time. Although both are of similar quality, the demand for the latter is greater. The artificially fermented tea becomes more stable in its property after a little storage and is a good choice for a daily drink.

High-quality dry processed tea is brownish-red or deep maroon. The tea liquid is clear and dark red. The taste is smooth and mellow with a sweet aftertaste. The processed tea is mild and most suitable for middle-aged and senior tea drinkers. It is also good for people with digestive problems, high cholesterol or blood pressure.

▲ Processed Pu-erh tea cake

▲ Processed Pu-erh tea liquid

2. According to the shape: compressed tea and loose tea

Compressed tea

Pu-erh tea is usually compressed into cakes, bowls, bricks, etc.

Tea cakes packaged into piles of seven are called seven-cake tea. In olden times, one cake weighed 400g, and forty-two cakes were put into a bamboo basket. This number was determined by the height of horses for transportation and the size of the bamboo baskets. Today, most cakes weigh 357g each and 84 cakes make a basket. There are also 200g, 250g, 500g and 3000g cakes in the market.

Pu-erh tea compressed into the shape of bowls is called bowl tea. There are 100g, 250g and 500g tea bowls in the market. You may also find smaller ones of 5g or 10g.

Pu-erh tea in the shape of bricks is called brick tea. In addition, you will find heart-, pagoda-, pumpkin- and mushroom-shaped compressed tea. Quality compressed Pu-erh tea is the same color as loose tea. It is compactly packed with distinct edges and corners, and has a smooth and even surface.

▲ Gourd-shaped Pu-erh

▲ Cake-shaped Pu-erh tea

▲ Bowl-shaped Pu-erh tea

▲ Brick-shaped Pu-erh tea

Mold for making brick-shaped tea at Yiwu, used by even third generation of tea producers of today

▼ A couple appreciating tea (carving)

Loose Pu-erh tea

Raw tea and processed tea are both called loose tea before being compressed. There are many kinds of sun-baked green crude loose tea. Processed loose tea includes Jinya (golden sprout), Gongting (imperial) Pu-erh (now denoting a grade of the raw material, details will be given later), and other kinds of loose tea.

▲ Loose Pu-erh tea

II. Other Classifications of Pu-erh Tea

1. According to the picking season: three-season tea or batch tea

Generally, Pu-erh tea is produced in the same seasons as other kinds of tea. Thus, Pu-erh tea is also classified into spring tea, summer tea and autumn tea according to the season when leaves are picked.

In Yunnan, tea farmers classify the periods for picking tea into batches. The first and second batches of tea are spring tea, the third and fourth batches are summer tea and the fifth and the later batch are autumn tea (also called cereal flower tea), among which spring tea and cereal flower tea tastes best.

The above classification only applies to arbor tea. Modern technology has been applied to increase production of tea. This has impacted the traditional tea-leaf picking timing.

2. According to the type and age of the tea tree: arbor tea and terrace tea, etc.

We find words such as "arbor tea" and "ancient arbor tea" on packages of Pu-erh tea and also hear terms like "terrace tea" and "wild ancient arbor tea." All these terms are related to the type and age of the source tree of the tea.

Arbor tea

All the tea trees evolved from the tea trees with high trunks in south Yunnan. They were planted in the north, east and south via different routes. As the temperature and humidity were lower in their new growing places, they adapted to withstand these conditions. The tree leaves became smaller, and the trees finally were reduced to short bushes without trunks.

Arbor is a plant that has a tall trunk and branches in the shape of a crown high above the ground. It is commonly called a tree. Arbor tea is made from the fresh leaves picked from these trees in the Pu-erh tea-producing area in Yunnan.

Comparatively speaking, arbor tea depends on fewer artificial factors, such as fertilizer and pesticide than terrace tea. In other words, arbor tea is more ancient, ecological and healthy, and it can better satisfy the psychological and physical needs of modern times. However, it is more expensive than terrace tea.

▲ A sprout of the first-batch spring arbor tea

In the early morning, the first ray of sunlight shines through the fog on the ancient tea trees at Luoshuidong, Yiwu.

A sprout of the arbor tea tree

▲ A sprout of the terrace tea tree

Arbor tea leaves

▲ Terrace fresh tea leaves

Terrace tea garden

"Ancient arbor tea" specifies the age of the arbor tea. The full-grown trees are at least 100–200 years old. Therefore, ancient arbor tea leaves are picked from trees at least 200–300 years old. The high mountains in southwest Yunnan is the place of origin of tea trees. Before the "Cultural Revolution," there were 200- to 900-year-old ancient tea trees abounding in the region producing Pu-erh tea (the six major tea-producing mountains in ancient and modern times). Subsequently, to meet the growing demand, the tea farmers cut large numbers of ancient tea trees and let the short trees grow from the roots of these ancient tea trees, or they simply grew large areas of terrace tea trees to facilitate tea picking and management. Today, Yunnan tea gardens are similar to the tea gardens south of the Yangtze River. Many ancient tea trees, such as the King of the Bada wild tea tree which is 1,700 years old, the 800-year-old king of the transitional type in Nannuo Mountain and the huge 1,000-year-old tea gardens in Jingmai Mountain still remain. You can also find many ancient arbor tea gardens housing 200–300-year-old trees. There are different definitions of the "wild ancient arbor tea" in the tea industry. The "wild ancient arbor tea" is relative to the "modern managed terrace tea." According to the definition of "wild type-transitional type-planted type" in the academic world, there is virtually no real wild Pu-erh tea any more. Apart from wild arbor tea trees, there are also wild bush tea trees.

Terrace tea trees

Terrace tea trees are planted tea bushes. Constant tea picking and trimming, keep these trees short. They are densely planted with little space for them to spread. Such tea trees are characterized by small thin leaves, and their sun-baked green crude tea striations are also delicate. Terrace tea trees are also known as base tea trees or garden tea trees.

Tea farmers cultivate the land on the mountain slopes and plant tea trees on the terraced slope, giving the name "terrace tea." The arbor tea trees are older than terrace tea trees and their extract is also different. The differences in the place of origin of the raw materials, processing, storage environment and pile fermentation technology have a direct influence on the quality of Pu-erh tea, lending the subtle differences in the tea liquids. However, the differences do not indicate superiority of one over the other.

The words "ancient arbor tea" bring to mind a sense of purity and closeness with nature. For this, arbor tea commands a higher price than terrace tea. However, this does not signify its superiority, because both have their own characteristics. Drinkers can choose according to their preference.

▲ A couple preparing mountain terrace to plant terrace tea trees

3. According to the storage environment: dryly stored tea and damply stored tea

Dry storage and damp storage are relative. The fermentation of Pu-erh tea requires predefined temperature and humidity. The naturally stored and fermented tea is called dryly stored tea. Tea placed in an artificial environment, with higher temperature and humidity to hasten the fermentation process, is called damply stored tea.

Dryly stored tea is not necessarily of high quality or damply stored tea necessarily inferior because storage condition is merely one of many factors affecting the quality of tea. Damp storage makes the raw tea age quickly. Mostly used by tea traders to simulate the natural fermentation process in shorter time, some even pass off damply stored tea as naturally fermented tea. Although wet storage facilitates faster fermentation, tea may become moldy if handled improperly. Thus, damply stored tea is not popular as moldy tea affects people's appetite. There is no unified standard for the correct fermentation of Pu-erh tea. As long as the tea is kept from becoming moldy and acquires fragrance and taste, all methods are acceptable.

Dryly stored Pu-erh tea

High-quality dryly stored raw Pu-erh tea has distinct striations. Its color varies from brownish-green to brownish-red and its fragrance is rich and pure. Depending on the storage time, the tea liquid deepens from reddish-orange to crimson similar to the color of red wine. The taste is mellow and smooth. The soaked tea leaves are tougher than those of damply stored tea.

Dryly stored processed tea is brownish-red when it is dry, its tea liquid bright red and clear. The color lightens after several brews and it is advisable to boil the tea after steeping it three or four times. As processed tea is completely post-fermented tea, there is no need to further store it. Sell or drink it immediately.

▲ Brewed leaves of dryly stored raw tea

▲ Dryly stored raw tea liquid

▲ Dryly stored raw tea cake

Damply stored Pu-erh tea

If stored properly, damply stored Pu-erh tea will taste no different from other kinds of processed tea though it is often associated with moldy and poor-quality tea. The moldy tea is dark in color with a distinct damp or even moldy smell.

The tea liquid is also dark like soy sauce. The soaked tea leaves are decayed and irritating to the throat. Such kind of tea may adversely affect health and should be avoided.

▲ Brewed leaves of damply stored tea

▲ Damply stored tea liquid

▲ Damply stored tea cake

4. According to the tenderness of raw material: different grades

But for the historical imperial tribute tea made from choicest tender leaves, large batches of Pu-erh tea are made from coarse and old tea leaves. Today, Pu-erh tea is classified according to the grades of its raw materials. The higher-grade Pu-erh tea composition has more tender sprouts and tastes milder and sweeter, while the lower-grade tea has more stems and a stronger flavor.

▲ Tea cakes from tender leaves   ▲ Tea cakes with thick and strong leaves

In the past, Tibetans in the major Pu-erh tea consuming areas favored the coarse and old tea. It is hard to tell which kind of tea is better. Their tastes are just different from each other.

5. According to the number of material types: single material and assorted materials

In the past, considering its cost and flavor, while compressing, the tender and well-preserved tea leaves were put at the bottom of the cotton bags and the tea leaves of lower quality were put on top. The tea cakes compressed in this way had clear and well-distributed stripes on one surface to make them look better. There was a distinct difference between the contents and the surface. Sometimes such tea cakes contained three to four layers of leaves of different qualities. In the past, this tea was produced mainly to lower prices.

Today, in addition to the Pu-erh tea made from a single material, there is also tea made from raw materials of different grades. The reasons for the latter are threefold. First, to highlight the thick striations of the big-leaf tea. Secondly, to leverage the quality and taste of different kinds of Pu-erh tea. For example, the tender tea leaves and coarse and old tea leaves compressed together in layers giving different taste, such as freshness, sweetness, mellowness and richness. Thirdly, to sell poor-quality tea at a high price. For example, raw tea not stored for long and artificially fermented tea are compressed together to simulate the taste and color of the tea naturally fermented for 3–5 years and sell it at a premium. Assortment is a traditional way to enrich the quality of Pu-erh tea. There are professionals for such assortment who can make assorted tea cake based on the characteristics and qualities of sun-baked green crude tea of different ages and grades. Such assorted tea is bright red in color with a mellow taste.

6. According to the processing tool: handmade tea and machine-made tea

In traditional tea production, heating, twisting, drying and compressing are all done manually. In modern production, except for the selection, everything is done by machines.

Handmade tea

After completing all the other processing steps, tea leaves are manually compressed into different shapes under the weight of a pressing stone. The pressing stone is a traditional tool used for compressing tea leaves much before the iron pressing machine was invented. The stone is of different shapes and specifications. Cakes compressed by the stones are neat and simple in shape.

▲ Tea leaves being compressed manually

Machine-made tea

Machine-made tea first appeared in the 1950s. Machines can heat, twist, dry, etc. Tea cakes compressed by machines are harder and their fermentation is slower but they are easy to preserve.

▲ Heater for machine-made tea

▲ Withering platform for machine-made tea (with ventilators inside)

▲ Twisting machine

7. According to preservation time: raw tea and old tea

We have learned about raw tea, but what is old tea? Most buyers of naturally fermented tea will ask tea sellers for "old tea."

People call the raw tea preserved for a period of time by different names, which often leads to confusion. We often come across confusing conversation such as "Is this old tea?" "No, it is raw tea." "Is it? But is it fermented!" "Oh, this is five-year raw tea!" "Oh, five-year old tea!"….

Some people call all the Pu-erh tea preserved for a certain period of time "old tea"; some call naturally preserved Pu-erh tea (and other post-fermented dark tea) "old tea" and preserved processed tea "old preserved tea"; and still others call all the naturally preserved tea "raw tea," irrespective of the fact that it has been preserved for 3 years or 10 years. Be it raw or ripe, within a certain period of time, its quality will not degrade, rather slightly improve and become better. This is the biggest difference between Pu-erh tea and other kinds of tea.

 For other kinds of tea, "old preserved tea" is the blanket name for old, outdated and stale tea. Except for some types of Pu-erh tea, Oolong tea and black tea, other types of tea are considered better and more valuable when fresh. These types of tea cannot endure time. After only one year, they become "old preserved tea," when the dry tea loses color and becomes dry. This is especially true of green tea, which turns from green to yellow or brown and loses fragrance if stored for long. When the tea is brewed, its fragrance is light and impure. The tea liquid is dark, tastes stale and weak. The soaked leaves are dark yellow and twisted. Because the "old preserved tea" is stale and tastes bad, people prefer fresh tea. When referring to Pu-erh tea avoid using the term "old preserved tea;" say "preserved tea."

8. According to function: tea for drinking and tea for ornamentation

It is easy to understand tea for drinking. Tea for ornamentation is rarely seen in other types of tea. This use is unique to Pu-erh tea.

Pu-erh tea is made into ornaments ranging from small accessories to big plaques. In the Pu-erh producing and selling areas, you can find various ornaments made from Pu-erh tea, but the raw materials used are usually of inferior quality. Such tea is purely ornamental and not to be consumed.

Part 3

Brewing Pu-erh Tea

There are many ways to brew Pu-erh tea: baking it on fire, make it in earthen teapots or boiling over a stove. There is Pu-erh tea flavored with milk or with chrysanthemum. There is also instant Pu-erh tea for office goers. Ways of making Pu-erh tea are as varied as those of other types of tea.

I. Preparations for Making Pu-erh Tea

According to the Chinese way of tea making, the kind of containers and types of tea brewed may vary; in order to have a cup of fragrant tea, good tea leaves, fresh water, appropriate water temperature and timing are key. The following are the major steps for making tea:

Clean and warm the containers: Warm the kettle and cups by pouring boiling water.

Add tea leaves: Take out the adequate amount of tea leaves from the tea-leaf container and put them in the teapot or cups.

Brew the tea: Pour water (80–100°) onto the tea leaves and steep.

Savor the tea: Pour the tea liquid in a cup to drink it or directly drink from the cups or teapot where the tea is brewed.

The steps for making Pu-erh tea is not different from making other kinds of tea. The difference lies in the special quality and form of Pu-erh tea. Compressed Pu-erh tea should be loosened and "woken up" for a while. Pu-erh tea is slightly different from other types of tea in terms of preparing tea leaves and tools, amount of leaves needed, water temperature and timing.

▲ Appreciating tea

(I) Preparing Tea Leaves

1. Loosening compressed tea

Pu-erh tea is known as the seven-cake tea. Although we find loose Pu-erh tea, it is best preserved in the shape of cakes. So most types of Pu-erh tea are in tea cakes. Loose tea leaves can be used to make tea directly but the compressed leaves must be first loosened.

Loosen the tea with a tea knife: If the compressed tea cake is not too hard, then shake or poke lightly and tea leaves will separate. If it is hard, loosen it with a knife specially made for loosening compressed tea. Start from the relatively loose part at

▲ Loosening tea leaves

the corners of the cake, insert the knife, gently prize and loosen the leaves and put them into the tea holder for use. It is simple and convenient to loosen compressed tea leaves with a tea knife but the leaves break easily.

Loosen the tea by steaming: Before compressing, the leaves were steamed to soften them. Now too, we can steam the cake to loosen the leaves without damaging the leaves. This is a little more complicated than loosening the leaves with the tea knife.

Irrespective of the kind of pot used, the method is similar: Steam the cake and take it out when it expands and loosen it with hand or knife while it is hot. It is much easier to loosen the whole cake, and the leaves remain unbroken.

▲ Loosening compressed tea leaves by steaming

But if there is leftover tea after use, dry the loosened tea before putting away. According to some, the leaves loosened by steaming are less fresh.

But different people have different feelings about such subtle details.

Waking up loose tea: The well-preserved loose tea should be exposed to the air before being brewed. This is called "waking up the tea," after which, the tea smells more fragrant and tastes mellower. This is similar to letting red wine breathe to enhance its taste.

After waking up the leaves, put adequate leaves into the tea holder for use.

▲ Waking up tea leaves

2. Quantity of leaves

The quantity of leaves needed varies according to individual preference, the brewing method, the size of tools and the characteristics of the tea.

Usually the ratio between the amount of tea leaves and water is 1:40 or 1:45, but this can be adjusted according to different tastes. For example, in Hong Kong, Taiwan, Fujian, Guangdong and Guangxi, people love strong tea so more leaves can be added, while northern people are fond of weak tea so the quantity of leaves can be reduced. The amount of tea needed also varies according to the characteristics of the tea. For example, processed tea, raw tea and old tea (including raw tea preserved for a certain period of time) need varying amount of leaves. As different types of Pu-erh tea have different raw materials, processing techniques, preserving conditions and storage time, we should not be dogmatic in terms of the amount of tea leaves needed.

(II) Preparing Tea Ware

Tea ware is the most important aspect in the making of tea. One characteristic of the Oolong tea lies in its special tea ware. In the past, there was no special tea ware for making and appreciating Pu-erh tea. People chose tea ware according to their likes.

In recent years, some conventions have been formed to help choose tea ware for Pu-erh tea. For example, for raw Pu-erh tea, choose tea ware that is used for brewing the slightly fermented Oolong tea.

For processed tea and old tea, choose purple-clay ware or cups with a porcelain surface. Bright red Pu-erh tea liquid is complemented by white porcelain cups or porcelain and purple-clay cups with white glazed lining. The volume of the cup can be similar or bigger than that of the cup used for Oolong tea.

Some people use glassware with containers inside to make Pu-erh tea. They are convenient and fashionable.

It is not essential to use the entire set of porcelain, purple-clay or other ware. Tea ware of different materials can be mixed and used in combination. For example, a purple-clay teapot with porcelain teacups, a porcelain-covered teacup with purple-clay cups can be put together. A glass fairness cup can be added to the above combination. Or glass-covered cups can be used with tea ware of other materials to highlight the bright red tea liquid.

Other complementary wares include ceremony tea ware, tea cloth, water bowl and strainer, among which the last is a necessary tool.

And don't forget the tea knife for loosening tea cakes.

Besides, the harmonious coexistence of the various ethnic groups such as Dai, Hani, Blang and Jinuo in the Pu-erh tea-producing areas, who have been picking and producing Pu-erh tea for generations, has developed many unique and primitive tea appreciation methods. The handmade pottery tea ware is traditional and simple. With such special ware, we can better appreciate the fragrance and natural tough spirit of the tea.

Tea drinkers can mix and match tea ware according to their tastes and the characteristics of the types of Pu-erh tea.

Next, let us learn about the major types of wares used for making and appreciating Pu-erh tea.

1. Boiling kettle

In the present times, the convenient electric kettle is most popular. The ideal way for making quality Pu-erh tea is to use a pottery kettle to boil spring water from the mountain. Water boiled in pottery or copper kettles over fire will surely add to the flavor of the tea. But before being used, the newly bought pottery kettles should be cleaned and rid of the earthen smell, first with clean water, and then with boiled water twice.

▲ Electric porcelain kettle

▲ Electric kettle

▲ Glass kettle

▲ Pottery kettle

2. Tea ware

Use pottery, porcelain, glass teapot and covered teacups for brewing Pu-erh tea.

Purple-clay teapot

Yixing purple-clay teapot is the first choice for making Pu-erh tea. Purple-clay teapots are air permeable, absorbent and preserve heat. They preserve the fragrance and taste of the tea well. Use round, thick-walled, rough-sanded purple-clay teapots, which allow tea liquid to flow smoothly, to make processed tea and preserved raw tea. Such pots reduce the smell of pile fermentation of processed tea and the moldy smell of old tea. With proper care, purple-clay teapots can enhance the fragrance and mellowness of the Pu-erh tea over time.

Contrary to the small teapots best for Oolong tea, bigger ones should be used to make Pu-erh tea. For two to three drinkers, a purple-clay teapot of 250ml is good. And for more people, larger teapots can be chosen. The best choice is a pot with good heat dissipation property and a wide mouth allowing easy flow of the tea liquid.

Newly bought teapots (not those that have been used before sale) should be cleaned by boiling pure water or tea liquid to get rid of the typical smell of the kiln or earth. It is better to use the new pots for some time before making good tea in it. This ensures the teapots and the tea

▲ Various purple-clay teapots

complement each other. Besides, porcelain teapots and covered teacups can also be used to make tea.

Covered tea bowls

Covered tea bowls are convenient to use and are a good choice to make various kinds of tea. Astute shopkeepers often use them to make sample tea so that the buyers can taste the tea, smell the fragrance and see the dry leaves absorb the water.

Due to the easy appreciation of the change in the tea liquid in the covered tea bowls, their visual appeal and their practical purpose, covered tea bowls, especially those made of porcelain, are often used in making Pu-erh tea.

▲ Porcelain-covered tea bowl with painting

Be careful about the quantity of tea leaves and water needed to avoid spilling while brewing.
Avoid scalding.

▲ Blue-and-white porcelain-covered tea bowl

▲ Porcelain-covered tea bowl with hand-painted lotus

▲ Glass-covered tea bowl

3. Teacups

Teacups of different materials can be used for common use. But bigger ones are better.

These days you find a wide-mouthed teacup bigger than the Gong Fu teacup with a volume of 200ml. This shows Pu-erh tea should be appreciated in big teacups. The thick, wide-mouthed teacup complements the mild, mellow and primitive rough taste of Pu-erh tea.

White porcelain or celadon cups enhances the appreciation of the color of the Pu-erh tea liquid. Glass cups are also good.

▲ Hand-painted teacup

▲ Glass teacup

▲ Pu-erh teacup

▲ Celadon teacup

▲ Blue-and-white porcelain teacup

▲ Purple-clay teacup

4. Fairness cups (Gongdao Bei)

Pu-erh tea is famous for its bright and colorful tea liquid. People often compare its color to preserved red wine, amber, garnet and ruby, etc. The tea color is like a rainbow ending in the fairness cup, making the glass fairness cup the first choice for tea making. White porcelain fairness cup is also very popular.

▲ Porcelain fairness cup   ▲ Painted porcelain fairness cup

▲ Pottery fairness cup   ▲ Glass fairness cup

▲ Purple-clay fairness cup   ▲ Porcelain fairness cup

5. Ethnic Pu-erh tea ware

Ethnic tea ware includes tea-baking jars and earthen pots, etc. Those from the Pu-erh tea-producing areas in Yunnan give the tea a primitive and natural taste.

▲ Tea-baking jar

6. Other complementary tea ware

There are many complementary tea ware, such as the kettle stand, the strainer, the tea cloth, the teaspoon, etc. Making Pu-erh tea is a quiet and joyous process.

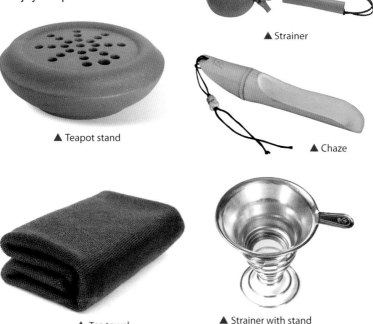

▲ Strainer

▲ Teapot stand

▲ Chaze

▲ Tea towel

▲ Strainer with stand

There is no single unified principle of choosing tea ware for making the tea. As long as it suits the characteristics of the tea and the drinker, it is good tea ware.

(III) Water and Its Temperature

Just as tea ware is an important aspect of tea making, water is equally so because no tea can be made without water. The quality of water is key to the taste of the tea liquid.

People down the ages have left many incisive comments on water for making tea. "The quality of tea depends on the water. Good tea made with excellent water becomes excellent, while excellent tea made with good water is only good." This is also true for Pu-erh tea. There are people who go to the extent of fetching water from mountain springs in order to make tea with its sweet water. It requires special abilities and also offers great pleasure to appreciate the subtle differences in the tea made from different types of water. The best choice is the mountain spring water, which, after being nourished in the pottery jar, will give the Pu-erh tea a mellower taste.

Usually pure water and mineral water is used to make Pu-erh tea. Potable tap water can also be used, but it is better to leave the water in a container for a day and a night to disperse the chlorine before using it to make tea.

The temperature of the water depends on the type of tea. When brewing Pu-erh tea made of tender buds like the Gongting (Imperial) Pu-erh Tea Cake and Nv'er (Maiden) Tribute Tea Cakes from the Menghai Tea Factory, the water should cool down a little after being boiled to avoid scorching the tender leaves. But for other types of Pu-erh tea cakes and tea bricks, it is better to use boiling water.

(IV) Making Pu-erh Tea

1. Special tools—tea knife and strainer

Tea knife (also Pu-erh knife), a tool in the shape of knife made of ox bone or horn, hard wood or stainless steel, is used to loosen compressed tea as mentioned before. It can be found in places where Pu-erh tea is sold.

Pu-erh tea, especially the fermented and compressed tea, has to be loosened with the Pu-erh knife before being brewed. There will be some tea grounds in the tea liquid, so it is better to filter the grounds before drinking. Thus, a strainer is more important in Pu-erh tea making than in making other kinds of tea.

▲ Pu-erh knives

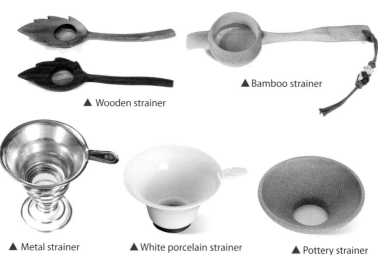

▲ Wooden strainer

▲ Bamboo strainer

▲ Metal strainer

▲ White porcelain strainer

▲ Pottery strainer

2. An indispensable step—soaking tea

Brew Pu-erh tea in boiling water. Pour boiling water on the tea and then pour the water out immediately. Repeat once or twice in quick succession to prevent the tea substances from dissolving in the water, which may affect the taste of the tea liquid. This is called "soaking the tea." To "soak tea" is also known as "to wash tea." Careful drinkers will wash whichever kind of tea they drink.

There are many steps in making Pu-erh tea and they all involve time. The longer the tea is stored, the more likely they will be polluted with dust and dirt. Although soaking tea can wash the dust off, high-quality Pu-erh tea should not be soaked long or repeatedly in hot water.

Soaking tea can help loosen the lumps of stored-for-long and compressed tea. For old tea which has been stored for many years, soaking can also get rid of the strange smell and wake up the dormant tea. Therefore, soaking is an indispensable step in making tea.

II. Pu-erh Tea & City Dwellers

For hundreds of years, Pu-erh tea has been the daily necessity for and treasured as life by the Tibetans. In the mid-Qing Dynasty when Pu-erh tea became the imperial tribute, it was sought after by senior government officials and rich people.

Today in the 21st century, Pu-erh tea has become part of modern life.

The great increase in material wealth, the fast pace of living and the unprecedented pressure from work has left modern city dwellers in a state of health featuring over-nutrition, lack of exercise and mental stress. To combat ailments arising from this lifestyle, people have turned to mild, healthy and green food and drink. Pu-erh tea is just such a kind of refreshing drink. Therefore, there is a craze for Pu-erh tea across China. Among all kinds of tea, Pu-erh tea, both in terms of its growth environment and health-preserving effect, is fitting for modern people. Its effect in lowering cholestrol and regulating digestion is a favorite topic among its fans. Pu-erh tea has quickly become synonymous with fashion, nature and health.

Today, whether it is a party among relatives or friends, or a business meeting, a sharing of Pu-erh tea with its fragrance and sweetness brings great pleasure to the body and mind.

Pu-erh tea has already entrenched itself in people's heart and become a new force on the tea market.

(I) Making Raw Pu-erh Tea

Pu-erh tea that has been preserved for few years is close to green tea in its properties and color. Its taste is sweet tinged with a little bitterness. Its fragrance is pure and mild and lingers even after the tea is finished. While brewing raw tea, lower the water temperature. Serve immediately after pouring to avoid scorching the leaves and tainting the tea liquid with that smell.

Pre-brewing Preparations

Tea ware: Electric tea kettle, covered tea bowl, fairness cup, teacup, tea holder, strainer, water bowl, Pu-erh knife, teaspoon, etc.
Water: Pour enough water in the electric tea kettle and bring to boil.
Tea leaves: Raw Pu-erh tea.

▲ Tea holder

▲ Covered tea bowl

▲ Fairness cup

▲ Strainer

▲ Teacup

▲ Water bowl

▲ Teaspoon

▲ Pu-erh knife

1. Prize the tea: Use tea knife to prize adequate raw tea gently without grounding the leaves.

2. Prepare tea leaves: Put the leaves in the tea holder for later use.

3. Warm the covered tea bowl: Pour boiling water in the tea bowl.

4. Warm the fairness cup: Pour the water from the covered tea bowl into the fairness cup.

5. Warm the strainer: Warm the strainer with the hot water from the fairness cup.

6. Warm the teacups: Clean and warm the teacups with the hot water from the mug.

7. Drain water: Drain the water from the teacups into the water bowl.

8. Put leaves: Put the leaves in the covered tea bowl.

9. Soak leaves: Pour boiling water into the covered tea bowl as shown.

10. Drain water: Drain the water quickly into the water bowl.

11. Make tea: Pour boiling water into the covered tea bowl along its inside.

12. Cover the tea bowl: Replace the lid.

13. Place the strainer: While leaves are brewing, place the strainer on the fairness cup.

14. Pour the tea liquid: Pour the hot tea liquid into the fairness cup.

15. Empty the tea liquid: Empty the tea liquid in the covered tea bowl.

16. Distribute the tea: Fill the tea cups up to 70%.

17. Clean the tea stains: Clean the fairness cup after every use.

18. Appreciate the tea: Invite guests to appreciate the tea in the teacups.

TIPS

Things to remember while making tea:

First, when loosening the tea cake, start from the relatively loose part and loosen the cake along the striations in the tea leaves to break fewer leaves.

Secondly, use the strainer to make the tea liquid brighter and cleaner by filtering out the grounds of compressed tea.

Third, be sure to pour all the tea liquid out and avoid soaking of the leaves for long to avoid affecting the flavor of the next brew of tea. Open the lid to dissipate the heat.

(II) Making Processed Pu-erh Tea (Loose Tea)

When making artificially fermented processed tea, the most important point is the appropriate time for pouring water in and draining it out.

After putting in adequate tea leaves, slowly pour the hot water. Quickly drain out the tea liquid so that it tastes smooth and mellow.

Pre-brewing Preparations

Tea ware: Electric tea kettle, purple-clay teapot, fairness cup, strainer, teacup, tea holder, tea funnel, etc.
Water: Pour enough water into the electric tea kettle and bring to boil.
Tea leaves: Processed Pu-erh tea (loose tea).

▲ Purple-clay teapot

▲ Fairness cup

▲ Tea funnel

▲ Water bowl

▲ Chaze

▲ Teacup

▲ Tea holder

1. Taking out the tea leaves: Use the small tea holder to take out loose tea from the pottery tea container. Place it in the big tea holder.

2. Observe the tea leaves: Loose tea leaves have not been compressed or loosened, so it is unbroken.

3. Warm the teapot: Pour boiling water in the teapot.

4. Warm the fairness cup: Pour the water from the teapot into the fairness cup.

5. Warm the teacups: Warm the teacups with the hot water from the mug.

6. Drain water: Drain the water from the teacups into the water bowl.

7. Adding tea leaves: Place the tea funnel on the mouth of the teapot and put adequate leaves.

8. Soaking leaves: Pour boiling water in the teapot to soak the leaves.

9. Skim the foam: Skim the foam from the mouth of the teapot and replace the lid.

10. Drain water: Drain the water quickly into the water bowl.

11. Brew the tea: Pour the boiling water in along the inside of the teapot and replace the lid.

12. Pouring the tea liquid: Pour the hot tea liquid quickly into the fairness cup through the strainer.

13. Empty the teapot: Pour out all the tea liquid from the teapot.

14. Distribute the tea: Pour the tea liquid from the mug into the teacups evenly.

15. Serve the tea: Serve the tea with both hands to the guests.

TIPS

Wash the processed tea and pour the tea liquid out quickly. Slowness will make the tea bitter and the color dark. Boiling water should be slowly poured into the teapot along its inside to avoid stirring the leaves too much so that several brews of the tea liquid can be of similar taste, color and strength.

(III) Making "Crab Pincers" Tea

"Crab pincers" is a kind of parasite growing on the several-hundred-year-old ancient arbor tea trees. Although not really Pu-erh tea, it is closely related to Pu-erh tea, having its own characteristics (detailed introduction on page 138).

Pre-brewing Preparations

Tea ware: Set of pottery tea ware, strainer, teacups, fairness cup, water bowl, etc.
Water: Fill the electric tea kettle with sufficient water and bring to boil.
Tea leaves: Crab pincers.

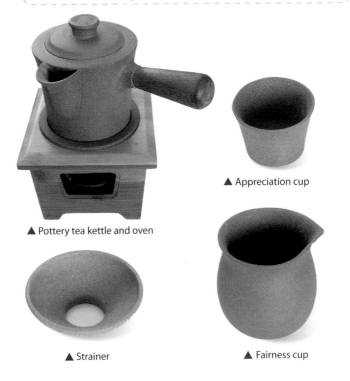

▲ Pottery tea kettle and oven

▲ Appreciation cup

▲ Strainer

▲ Fairness cup

Brewing

1. Warm the kettle: Pour the boiling water into the pottery kettle.

2. Warm the fairness cup: Pour the water from the pottery kettle into the fairness cup.

3. Warm the teacups: Pour the water from the fairness cup into the teacups.

4. Drain the water: Drain the water from the teacups into the water bowl.

5. Take out the "tea" (crab pincer): Take out an adequate amount of crab pincers.

6. Adding "tea leaves" in: Add the crab pincers into the kettle.

7. Soak "tea leaves": Pour boiling water into the pottery tea kettle to soak the crab pincers.

8. Drain the water out: Drain the water into the water bowl.

9. Pour the water: Pour the boiling water into the kettle.

10. Boil the "tea": Place the kettle over a lit stove.

11. Make tea: Bring the tea liquid to boil.

12. Pour the tea liquid: Place the strainer on the fairness cup and pour the tea liquid into the mug.

13. Distribute the tea: Divide the tea liquid from the mug and into the teacups equally.

14. Serve the tea: The tea liquid of crab pincers is sweet and refreshing with a light medicinal fragrance.

▲ Crab pincers preserved for some time, turning brownish-red

(IV) Making Old Paka Tea

"Old paka," meaning "old leaves" is a special kind of Pu-erh tea commonly used by the ethnic minorities in Yunnan. It is seldom sold in the market. The correct way to enjoy its fragrance is by boiling the tea liquid. (Detailed introduction on page 142).

Pre-brewing Preparations

Tea ware: Set of glass tea ware, electric tea kettle, tea tongs, bamboo teacups, etc.
Water: Fill the electric tea kettle with sufficient water and bring to boil.
Tea leaves: Old paka.

▲ Water bowl

▲ Glass tea kettle

▲ Tea tongs

▲ Bamboo teacup

▲ Old paka

1. Warm the kettle: Warm and wash the glass kettle with boiling water.

2. Drain the water: Drain the water from the glass kettle into the water bowl.

3. Adding tea leaves: Use tongs to add the old paka into the kettle.

4. Pour water: Fill the kettle up to 2/3 of its volume.

5. Light the stove: Light the fuel (candle or alcohol) and place the glass kettle on the stove.

6. Boil the tea: Bring it to boil.

7. Boil the tea: Once the tea liquid is boiling remove the kettle from the fire.

8. Smell the fragrance: Remove the lid and inhale the fragrance of old paka.

9. Distribute the tea liquid: Pour the boiled old paka tea liquid into the bamboo teacup.

10. Serve the tea: Serve the tea with both hands to the guests.

Old paka is a special type of tea in the Pu-erh tea family. Its details will be introduced later.

While boiling old paka, take out the leaves after you can smell the fragrance. The water will change color. Bamboo cups are not as good heat conductors as pottery and porcelain cups, so they should be cleaned beforehand and do not have to be warmed before pouring the tea.

Old paka leaves fully spread after being boiled.

(V) Making Tea with Crab Pincers Tea Liquid

Making the processed Pu-erh tea with Crab Pincers tea liquid can produce a special flavor. The processed Pu-erh gives out a deep fragrance while the Crab Pincers gives out a fresh one. Mixing the two brings out a unique strong and mellow taste.

Pre-brewing Preparations

Tea ware: Set of glass tea ware, purple-clay teacups, electric tea kettle, strainer, glass fairness cup, tea cloth.
Water: Fill sufficient water in the electric tea kettle and bring to boil.
Tea leaves: Brewed loose Pu-erh tea (processed tea).

▲ Dry crab pincers

▲ Strainer

▲ Glass tea kettle and stove

▲ Purple-clay teacup

1. Boil crab pincers: Boil crab pincers in the glass tea kettle.

2. Boil crab pincers: Boil them till they are bubbling in the water.

3. Prepare tea: Pick up the tea teapot.

4. Pour the tea liquid: Pour the crab pincers tea liquid into the purple-clay teapot.

5. Pour the tea liquid: Pour the tea liquid into the fairness cup through the strainer.

6. Distribute the tea: Distribute the tea liquid into the teacups.

7. Clean tea stains: Use the tea cloth to clean tea stains while distributing the tea liquid.

The crab pincers tea liquid can also be used to brew long-stored tea. The taste becomes mellower and more fragrant.

III. Ethnic Tea Art

Pu-erh tea's charm lies not only in its wonderful change of taste and its health benefits, but also in the ancient caravan tea route and the glamorous ethnic lifestyles in the tea-producing areas in Yunnan.

In the Pu-erh tea-producing areas live many ethnic groups, among whom the Hani, Dai, Blang and Yi have been tea farmers and producers for generations. Different ethnic groups follow different tea-making customs, and the most popular include baking the tea, dressing the cold tea with sauce and making instant thirst-quenching tea in bamboo tubes.

The ethnic groups in the tea-producing areas mainly drink sun-baked green crude tea, by brewing it in boiling water directly, brewing it after baking the tea in the pottery jar or boiling it in earthen pots.

They also use handy materials, such as plant tea bag for baked tea or the bamboo cup for boiled tea. There is Pu-erh tea wine made of tea liquid mixed with rice wine. In addition to drinking the tea, there are many other ways of enjoying Pu-erh tea. Jinuo people make interesting food preparations with tea and dress cold tea leaves with sauce and the Blang make bamboo tube acid tea, all of which are unique for they preserve the primitive and ancient tea-eating habits.

People in Simao and Dali like to drink pure or flavored baked tea made of the local green tea, bowl-shaped tea or tea cakes. While in northwest Yunnan and Tibet, one or more additional materials, such as butter (or other types of grease), milk, salt or even rice wine and roasted barley flour are added to the tea liquid to vary the flavor.

Baked Tea

Ethnic groups in the Pu-erh tea-producing areas usually use local earthen jars to bake sun-baked green crude tea till it acquires a scorched fragrance before brewing it.

The baked tea is the most popular drink. Given its rich fragrance and strong taste, baked tea is suitable for people who like strong tea.

Pre-brewing Preparations

Tea ware: Stove, boiling kettle, baking jar, tea funnel, teaspoon.
Water: Fill sufficient water in the electric tea kettle and bring it to boil.
Tea leaves: Loose Pu-erh tea (raw tea).

▲ Stove   ▲ Baking jar

▲ Tea funnel   ▲ Dry tea   ▲ Teacup

1. Baking jar: Light the stove and place the jar on the fire. Let it heat.

2. Place the tea funnel: Place the tea funnel on the jar. Take care not to get burned.

3. Adding tea leaves: Add the sun-baked green crude tea into the baking jar.

4. Bake the tea: Light the stove. Shake the jar periodically. Stop when you smell the burnt fragrance.

5. Pour water: Place the jar on the kettle stand and pour boiling water.

6. Wait a while: You will hear a crackling sound in the jar and see the leaves stir in the jar.

7. Pour the tea liquid: Distribute the tea liquid into the teacups.

8. Appreciate the tea: Baked tea is strong and bitter but has a lingering sweet aftertaste.

IV. Pu-erh Tea as a Daily Drink

Brew Pu-erh tea in a glass cup and experience the visual delight of the changing hues of the tea liquid—from bright, ruby red to old wine red to amber to agate red. Taste its mellowness that lingers on the tip of your tongue. At first sip, it is bitter but the second sip tastes sweet. Feel your fatigue and tiredness melt away.

When time is short, and when you do not have enough time to get together the purple-clay teapot, the fairness cup, the strainer and porcelain cups, just sit at your office desk and make a cup of instant tea; your mind will clear and the nerves relax. The paraphernalia is not important; what is more important is the tea!

Modern inventions have given us more options to make life simpler. You may choose a porcelain or purple-clay teapot with an inner container. The best inner container can be a glass or a transparent nontoxic plastic cup, both of which can be sealed. Press the button on the inner container to get tea. It functions like the teapot and you have a cup of strong red Pu-erh tea within minutes. Simple and trendy!

Making Pu-erh Tea in a Container inside a Teapot

Be it at home or in office, it is convenient and fashionable to make tea in the teapot holding a container.

Pre-brewing Preparations

Tea ware: Teapot (with a container inside), electric tea kettle.
Water: Fill the electric tea kettle with enough water and bring to boil.
Tea leaves: Loosened Pu-erh tea.

▲ Teapot holding a bottle inside.

▲ Loosened Pu-erh tea

▲ Water bowl

▲ Teacup

1. Warm the inner container: Pour boiling water into the inner container.

2. Warm the teapot: Press the button to let water flow out of the container into the teapot.

3. Drain water: Drain the water into the water bowl.

4. Adding tea leaves: Take out the inner container. Add the processed tea.

5. Replace the inner container: Replace the inner container inside the teapot.

6. Soak the leaves: Pour boiling water into the inner container.

7. Funnel the water: Cover the container and press the button to release the water into the teapot.

8. Drain water: Drain the water into the water bowl.

9. Make tea: Pour boiling water into the inner container.

10. Pour the tea liquid: Lift the inner container. Press the button to let the tea liquid flow into teapot.

11. Pour the tea liquid: Pour the tea into the teacups or directly drink from the container.

12. Appreciate the tea: The special teacup is a teapot and a fairness cup.

V. Flavored Pu-erh Tea

In the past, Pu-erh tea was known as "tea for the elderly," and today it is called "tea for women." One of the reasons for Pu-erh tea's great popularity is its health benefits.

According to research, tea was introduced to Tibet during the Tubo Regime. Living at an altitude above 3,000m, Tibetans lead a nomadic life, subsisting on beef, roasted qingke barley flour and highland barley, with very little vegetable and fruit. Tea with rich vitamins helps break down excessive fat in the human body. The importance of tea is evident in such Tibetan sayings as "Man can live without food for three days but can't live even one day without tea," "One day without tea gives man loose bowels and three days without tea makes him sick," and "Tea is blood! Tea is meat! Tea is life!" Buttered tea made from dark tea liquid helps Tibetans endure the tough environment on the plateau. In other words, buttered tea are complete meals for them.

Tea is not only indispensable to Tibetans, but also suitable for the modern city people who enjoy Pu-erh tea benefits for regulating body fat and digestion.

(I) Flavored Raw Tea with Processed Tea

There are two reasons for assorting raw Pu-erh tea with processed Pu-erh tea: tea manufacturers want to enrich the flavor of the tea by combining the sweetness and freshness of raw tea and the mellowness of processed tea; and some tea traders falsely sell the assorted tea to make profit.

This flavored tea offers the delicate and varying taste and flavor of the combination of different proportions of both types of tea.

Pre-brewing Preparations

Tea ware: Electric tea kettle, fairness cup, teacups.
Water: Fill the electric tea kettle with enough water and bring it to boil.
Tea: Tea liquid of raw tea and processed tea.

▲ Tea liquid of raw tea   ▲ Tea liquid of processed tea   ▲ Teacup

Brewing

1. Pour raw tea liquid: Pour raw tea liquid into the teacups to the level of 20%, 30%, 40% and 50% from Cup 1 to Cup 4 respectively.

2. Prepared raw tea liquid: Four cups with different amounts of raw tea liquid.

3. Pour processed tea liquid: Pour processed tea liquid to the level of 20%, 30%, 40% and 50% from Cup 4 to Cup 1 respectively.

4. Flavored tea liquid: This process shows the natural transition of dark to light color of the tea liquid. Enjoy!

(II) Pu-erh Tea with Milk (Flavored Tea)

This is a traditional as well as trendy way of enjoying Pu-erh tea. Like black tea, Pu-erh tea flavored with milk has a special taste.

Pre-brewing Preparations

Tea ware: Fairness cup, mixing glass, strainer, milk cup.
Ingredients: A cup of milk, a prepared cup of processed tea.

▲ Fairness cup

▲ Milk

▲ Mixing glass

▲ Strainer

Brewing

1. Pour tea liquid: Pour the prepared processed Pu-erh tea liquid into the fairness cup through the strainer.

2. Pour tea liquid: Pour the tea liquid from the fairness cup into the mixing glass.

3. Add milk: Add milk into the mixing glass to flavor the processed tea liquid.

4. Enjoy the tea: Pu-erh tea flavored with milk has a different taste from black tea with milk.

Pu-erh Tea with Chrysanthemum (Flavored Tea)

Pu-erh tea flavored with chrysanthemum is very popular in Guangdong and Guangxi. Some restaurants offer such tea only to special customers. To derive health benefits, you can also drink it daily.

Pre-brewing Preparations

Tea ware: Teacups, covered tea bowl, fairness cup, strainer.
Water: Fill the electric tea kettle with enough water and bring to boil.
Tea leaves: Loose Pu-erh tea (processed), chrysanthemum.

▲ Loose Pu-erh tea (processed)　　▲ Chrysanthemum　　▲ Strainer

▲ Teacup　　▲ Covered tea bowl　　▲ Fairness cup

1. Warm the covered tea bowl: Pour boiling water into the covered cup.

2. Warm the fairness cup: Pour the hot water from the covered cup into the fairness tea bowl.

3. Warm the teacups: Pour the hot water from the fairness cup into the teacups.

4. Drain the water: Drain the water from the teacups into the water bowl.

5. Take out the tea: Take out the processed Pu-erh tea from the bamboo tea container.

6. Add the tea: Add the tea into the covered teacup with the teaspoon.

7. Take out the chrysanthemum: Take out a suitable amount of chrysanthemum.

8. Add the chrysanthemum: Add the chrysanthemum into the covered tea bowl.

9. Soak the tea: Pour the boiling water into the covered tea bowl along its inside to soak the tea.

10. Drain the water: Drain the water for soaking the tea into the water bowl immediately.

11. Add boiling water: Pour the boiling water into the covered tea bowl.

12. Make tea: Pu-erh tea flavored with chrysanthemum is ready.

13. Place the strainer: Place the strainer on the fairness cup.

14. Pour the tea liquid: Pour the prepared tea liquid into the fairness cup.

15. Distribute the tea: Pour the tea from the fairness cup into each cup evenly.

16. Clean the tea stains: Clean the tea stains each time after pouring the tea.

Part 4

Appreciation of
Pu-erh Tea

Pu-erh tea can be divided into different categories according to its processing, grade of raw material, manufacturer, etc. Apart from the common types, there are some rare and special Pu-erh tea types. How do we differentiate the different types of Pu-erh tea?

I. Appreciation of Raw Pu-erh Tea

Parts 1 and 2 have discussed the definition of raw Pu-erh tea. Raw Pu-erh tea has strong tea property. It is richer and stronger in taste than the green tea processed from other kinds of tea. It tastes somewhat like Oolong tea.

The raw Pu-erh tea stored 5–10 years in natural conditions under suitable humidity and temperature, during which its strong tea property will mellow gradually, is the best. However, all types of raw tea do not necessarily benefit from storage and taste as good as the naturally fermented Pu-erh tea.

(I) Raw Cake Made from Tender Leaves

After the process of manual selection, shifting and compressing into tea cakes, 50kg quality sun-baked green crude yield only 500g tea shoot. The sample in the picture is the Nv'er (Maiden) Tribute Tea Cakes produced by Menghai Tea Factory, the best-quality representative traditional raw Pu-erh tea. Only one batch of such cakes were produced in 2004 and are now being fermented to various degrees.

This high-end raw Pu-erh tea is highly expensive and rarely available in north China.

TIPS
Menghai Tea Factory produced only one batch of the raw Nv'er (Maiden) Tribute Tea Cakes and the processed Gongting (Imperial) Pu-erh Tea Cakes, both of the best quality. Due to the fineness and tenderness of the raw material, the processed Gongting (Imperial) Pu-erh Tea Cakes were fermented to 70–80%. Because of the high standard of the raw material and the high cost selecting the material by hand, they have never been produced again. Scarcely seen in the market, they have become a collector's item.

Raw cakes made of fine and tender leaves ▲
Dry tea: Compact leaves, dark green color, fine tea hair visible

▲ Color and taste of tea liquid:
Clear, bright, yellowish-red; mellow and refreshing in taste; pure fragrance; endurable in hot water

▲ Brewed tea leaves: Fine, tender, yellowish-green, tough

(II) Arbor Tea

Yiwu is home to traditional Pu-erh tea (i.e., raw cakes), attracting lovers of Pu-erh tea from across the world. Being one of the main producers of quality Pu-erh tea raw material, Luoshuidong boasts large ancient tea gardens with 100–800-year old trees. The fresh tea leaves from the authentic wild ancient arbor trees are made into sun-baked green crude tea, which is extremely popular among tea traders especially from Hong Kong, Taiwan and South Korea. Traders often go to purchase the sun-baked green crude tea and even stay there to experience the process of picking and producing the tea. The raw tea cake shown below is from the wide ancient tea trees in Luoshuidong, Yiwu produced by Yiwu Baopuxuan Tea Factory. The tea leaves and shoots in the arbor tea cakes are stout with distinct, compact striations and visible white tea hair. The tea liquid has a rich and lasting fragrance. As the best of the quality Pu-erh tea, it is definitely the first choice from every perspective.

Normally reasonably priced, the wide arbor tea from Yiwu, Jingmai and Nannuo Mountains can be dear if its place of origin can be proven.

Wild ancient arbor tea commands high prices. Since 2007, the cost of the sun-baked green crude tea from the wild ancient arbor has been rising. For example, the price of the tea from Jingmai was 450 yuan/kg, while that from Yiwu reached 500 yuan/kg. Factories or traders then transported the tea to another place where it was processed and made into tea cakes of 357g each. The cost of raw

The fresh leaves of wide arbor tea are thick, rough, large and oval with pronounced stems and veins. Sun-baked green crude tea of this type has distinct striations, visible white hair and is bright in color. The tea liquid of arbor tea and that of raw terrace tea are both light yellow without obvious differences. However, arbor tea tastes sweet and is fragrant even after multiple brewing while the flavor of terrace tea is strong only in the first two brews.

Arbor tea from Yiwu ▲
Dry tea: Distinct compact striations, stout
shoots and leaves, visible white tea hair

▲ Color and taste of tea liquid:
Bright yellow, clear, fragrant,
mellow, sweet aftertaste

▲ Brewed leaves: Green, glossy,
unbroken

material was over 200 yuan. After adding cost of labor, transportation, packaging, marketing and sellers' profits, a real wild ancient arbor tea cake, origin well-known, would sell at 300 yuan at least. The purchase prices of sun-baked green crude tea from Mansong and Banzhang were even higher, at 2,000 yuan/kg and 1,000 yuan/kg respectively, because their annual yields were only 100kg and 500kg respectively.

To buy raw tea cakes means to enjoy their long history, clean environment and eco-friendly quality. Thus, it is important that their places of origin (e.g. Yiwu, Jingmai, Nannuo Mountains) should be authentic and they are made of authentic fresh wild arbor tea leaves. They should be priced reasonably. It is a great joy—whether you drink the tea yourself or add it into your collection.

The yield of wild ancient arbor tea is much lower than that of terrace tea. Take care to verify the authenticity of the tea. Keep the following three points in mind: (1) Terrace tea may be passed off as wild ancient arbor tea. (2) Sometimes only a small amount of wild ancient arbor tea is at the surface of the tea cake to camouflage the rest. (3) Summer arbor tea is passed off as spring arbor tea. The prices of these types of tea are similar to or lower than the price of the real wild ancient arbor tea.

Therefore, observe carefully to ensure that the tea possesses the following basic features of the wild ancient arbor tea. First, quality wild ancient arbor tea cakes retain shape with distinct and compact striations, fleshy shoots and leaves, and visible white tea hair. Second, the bright yellow tea liquid has a lingering rich fragrance and a sweet aftertaste. Third, the soaked leaves are green and glossy, with pronounced veins and prominent needle-like stems on the back, which makes the leaves look thick and solid—an important characteristic of wild ancient arbor tea.

The cultural relics market believes "the relic is fake if a part of it is fake." This applies to the wild ancient arbor tea. If in doubt about even a single point, don't buy the tea!

In large ancient tea gardens, some tall ancient trees have been cut while some new tea shoots are growing alongside, making it easier to pick tea leaves and maintain the new tea shoots. However, the sight of the stumps of the cut ancient trees causes people to sigh with disappointment.

Another early spring morning when the first rays of the sun bathe the ancient tea garden through the blooming cherry flowers. The tender and glossy arbor spring shoots are about to sprout.

(III) Quality Raw Tea Cake

The tea sample in the picture is Dayi No. 7432 Raw Tea Cake. Its flavor is enhanced when brewed in hot water. It can be stored for a long time. This was the first batch to have trade numbers.

The tea cakes sold in the year of manufacturing cost about 100 yuan each. After a three-year-storage, the price will rise to about 500 yuan each.

TIPS Trade number is also known as the tea number or the sales number. The first two numbers of the four-digit trade number represent the year of starting the processing. The third refers to the grade of its raw material while the last the code of the tea factory (1 for Kunming Tea Factory, 2 for Menghai Tea Factory, 3 for Xiaguan Tea Factory). In the trade number 7432, "74" represents the year 1974. The number 3 means that the raw material chosen is sun-baked green crude tea of grade 3, while 2 refers to Menghai Tea Factory.

▲ Dry tea from quality raw tea cakes

Quality raw Pu-erh tea cake ▲
Dry tea: Neat with fine compact striations
and tea hair, dark green and glossy

▲ Color and taste of tea liquid:
Golden, clear and bright; mellow
taste and sweet aftertaste with
light fragrance of glutinous rice;
qualities enhanced in hot water

▲ Brewed tea leaves: Green and
glossy, unbroken

(IV) Common Raw Tea Cake

The common terrace raw Pu-erh tea in the picture is from a tea market in Beijing. It was sold in its manufacturing year and each cake cost 95 yuan.

The tea leaves are relatively small and thin without visible tea hair and with delicate striations. Planted terrace tea trees are short without main stems as a result of frequent picking and trimming by man. Terrace tea trees are densely planted with little growth space.

 To differentiate terrace tea from arbor tea, observe the following. Color: Be it raw or processed tea, if the color of the dry tea leaves is sallow, dark and not bright, then it is probably terrace tea; arbor tea is likely to have silvery white tea hair. Brightness: Arbor tea is bright while terrace tea is dark. The central vein of soaked leaves: Break the leaf gently. If it feels tough, then it is arbor tea. If it feels fragile and tender, then it is terrace tea. As buyers, we need to taste the tea liquid before buying.

▲ Sun-baked green crude terrace tea

▲ Sun-baked green crude arbor tea

Common raw Pu-erh tea cakes ▲
Dry tea: Unbroken tea cake with
compact and distinct striations

▲ Color and taste of tea liquid:
Golden, clear, bitter, sweet
aftertaste

▲ Brewed tea leaves: Green and

II. Appreciation of Naturally Fermented Pu-erh Tea

Naturally fermented Pu-erh tea becomes more mellow and fragrant with time. The color and fragrance of the dry tea and the color and taste of the tea liquid also improve with age.

The tea liquid color varies according to the number of storage years. The dry Pu-erh tea produced and consumed the same year is fresh, jade green and glossy in color with a sun-baked smell. Its tea liquid is similar to green tea, mildly fragrant with a sweet aftertaste. Pu-erh tea naturally fermented for 5 years is apricot yellow in color with a rich, lingering fragrance, mellow taste and a sweet and pleasant aftertaste. Dry Pu-erh tea, fermented naturally for 10–20 years, is the same as the tea processed with pile fermentation. Its tea liquid is bright red with a mellow and rich fragrance and flavor, gentle and refined taste and a sweet and pleasant aftertaste. However, the tea liquid of the 30-year-stored raw tea is similar to the tea naturally fermented for 5 years in terms of taste, color and fragrance.

(I) Five-year Tea Brick

Raw Pu-erh tea freshly produced without natural fermentation has a pungent taste. If the dry tea gradually turns brown and reddish, then the tea must have been stored in the north for at least 2 years. Pu-erh tea fermented for 3–5 years has a faint and pure fragrance. Its tea liquid is a clear light orange, fading after the third or fourth brew. If the tea liquid of the so-called 5-year tea is as red and bright as processed tea, then it may have been stored under special conditions instead of natural environment. The sample tea in the picture is from a time-honored shop in Yiwu.

Tea brick naturally fermented for 5 years from Yiwu ▲
Dry tea: Color turning brownish-red from dark green , striations are distinct

▲ Color and taste of tea liquid:
Bright red color, pure and rich
fragrance, mellow with a sweet
aftertaste and slightly pungent

▲ Brewed leaves: Reddish-brown,
relatively unbroken, flexible

(II) Ten-year Old Preserved Tea

This sample tea was bought from a Pu-erh tea market in Pu-erh County (now known as Ning'er County) 2 years ago.

The color of the 10-year dry tea is slightly darker than that of the 5-year tea and lighter than that of the 20-year tea stored in the same environment.

TIPS   It is commonly believed that the color of preserved tea will turn from light yellow (apricot yellow) to red and its tea liquid increasingly red with time. However, this is a fallacy. After the raw tea becomes old preserved tea after storing for about 30 years, the catechin oxide in the tea leaves gradually decay, and the tea liquid color returns to that of 5- to 10-year tea. Though the mellowness of the tea remains, its tea properties weaken.

10-year tea brick bought from Pu-erh County ▲
Dry tea: Brownish-red color, compact, distinct
striations

▲ Color and taste of tea liquid:
Bright red color, rich fragrance,
mellow taste, sweet aftertaste,
with almost no astringency

▲ Brewed leaves: Reddish-brown in
color, relatively unbroken

(III) Twenty-year-old Preserved Tea

The sample tea in the picture is from a local tea farmer in Jingmai. Collected from the tea trees in the huge ancient tea garden in Jingmai, the rough raw material is manually compressed into big tea bricks. The brick is not tightly compact, reddish-brown in color, mellow and rich in taste and endurable in hot water or even when being boiled.

TIPS Touch to feel the difference between the brewed leaves of the naturally fermented Pu-erh tea and the tea processed with pile fermentation. The tea leaf of the former may be broken but tougher and the vein and stem are relatively unbroken.

Twenty-year tea brick from Jingmai Mountain ▲
Dry tea: Some dark reddish-brown color striations
stick out like twisting tree roots

▲ Color and taste of tea liquid:
Dark red in the first brews and
lighter after 5–6 brews, bright red
after being boiled, rich in taste and
fragrant in smell, with a faint earthy
smell in the first 2–3 brews, but pure
in taste afterward

▲ Brewed leaves: Fragmented with
relatively unbroken tea stems
and veins and tougher than tea
processed with pile fermentation

III. Appreciation of Processed Pu-erh Tea

Processed Pu-erh tea is produced through pile fermentation, which accelerates the aging process. The quality of processed tea depends mainly on its raw material and the technique of pile fermentation. Almost all local households in the regions producing Pu-erh tea can make raw tea cakes; however, there is only one tea factory that manufactures processed tea across seasons under appropriate humidity, temperature and time using different raw materials. Therefore, the background information of the tea manufacturer is important to ensure the quality of the tea.

(I) Processed Cake Made from Tender Leaves

Pu-erh tea was listed as tribute tea by the imperial court during the reign of Emperor Yongzheng of the Qing Dynasty. Its production was supervised by the Pu-erh local government and it was transported to the capital by caravans. The "Gongting (Imperial) Pu-erh Tea," originally referred to as the "tribute Pu-erh tea to the imperial court," is today, Pu-erh tea of the best quality.

Gongting (imperial) loose Pu-erh tea can be commonly seen on the market; however, among the tea cakes, only the "Gongting (Imperial) Pu-erh Tea Cake" produced by Menghai Tea Factory is made according to strictest standard. The sample tea shown below is the rare "Gongting (Imperial) Pu-erh Tea Cake" produced in 2004 by Menghai Tea Factory. The "Gongting (Imperial) Pu-erh Tea Cake" follows a strict standard—only some 500g tea shoots is selected from every 50kg quality sun-baked green crude tea through manual selection and sifting.

TIPS Today, neither the "Nv'er (Maiden) Tribute Tea Cake" nor the "Gongting (Imperial) Pu-erh Tea Cake" is easily available, though any discussion about high-quality Pu-erh tea is incomplete without mentioning them. When buying "imperial" loose Pu-erh tea, trust your own senses and buy only after tasting it rather than being blinded by the "imperial" tag.

Gongting (Imperial) Pu-erh Tea Cake ▲
produced by Menghai Tea Factory
Dry tea: Neat and round in shape, with fine,
compact and tender striations, glossy color
and fine golden tea hair

▲ Color and taste of tea liquid:
Thick, dark red and bright, with
a mild taste, a sweet aftertaste
and misty on the surface. Mild
taste and rich and lingering
fragrance characterizes
Gongting (Imperial) Pu-erh Tea

▲ Brewed leaves: Reddish-brown,
tender tea shoots

(II) Processed Tea Cake with Camphorwood Flavor

Camphorwood-flavored Pu-erh tea is a favorite among tea lovers. According to experts, the camphorwood flavor can be added during the process of producing Pu-erh tea. Dry the rubbed and twisted raw tea over burning camphorwood. However, artificially generated camphorwood fragrance usually fades quickly. How do we get Pu-erh tea with lasting camphorwood fragrance?

The answer is planting camphor trees together with the tea trees. Sharing the same soil and root system, the tea leaves gradually imbibe the camphorwood fragrance. This fragrance remains even after the pile fermentation process.

Moreover, the fragrance of the camphor trees drives away harmful insects from the tea trees naturally, making the tea more ecologically friendly and safer. This type of tea is rarely seen in the domestic market and is chiefly exported to southeastern Asian countries. Produced according to specific requirements by some domestic tea traders, its price is high. The sample tea shown is the Zeng's processed tea produced by Mr. Zeng Yunrong, a tea expert enjoying Special State Allowance and the first Pu-erh tea expert to initiate the alternate planting of camphor trees and tea trees in the tea gardens.

▲ Loosened processed tea cake with camphorwood flavor

Camphorwood-flavored processed tea cake ▲
Dry tea: Compact and fleshy striations, similar
to other common processed tea cakes

▲ Brewed leaves: Brownish-red, glossy

▲ Color and taste of tea liquid:
   Dark red and bright, with a
   smooth taste, a sweet aftertaste
   and rich camphorwood fragrance

(III) Common Processed Tea (Lao Huang Pian)

The sample tea shown is from the Yunnan Simao tea market and priced at 80–100 yuan. It is one type of the common processed tea having features of quality-processed tea, such as relatively good flavor, pure fragrance and reasonable price.

> **TIPS** If you want Pu-erh tea only for consumption, then the reasonably priced tea with a good tea liquid color, taste and fragrance is the best choice for you.

Common processed Pu-erh tea brick from Yunnan Simao ▲
Dry tea: Reddish-brown with distinct striations, defined
edges and corners, suitable compactness

▲ Color and taste of tea liquid:
Dark red, mellow and rich in
fragrance, pure and smooth
in taste

▲ Brewed leaves: Reddish-brown

IV. Special "Pu-erh Tea"

Pu-erh tea has many fascinating differences compared to other kinds of tea. More and more people are discovering the uniqueness of "Pu-erh tea."

(I) Pu-erh Tea Paste

Almost on the verge of disappearing, Pu-erh tea paste used to be the special tribute to the Qing Dynasty imperial court. According to the *Supplement to the Compendium of Materia Medica,* Pu-erh tea paste is often pitch black; it is best known as an antidote to drunkenness and the green paste is especially good for improving digestion and reducing phlegm.

Having long lost its production technique, there are too few people left who know how to make it. Though highly exorbitant, its rarity makes it more sought after.

The tea paste in the picture below represents its original size and weighs about 300g. Made in April 2007 by Mr. Liu Zhan of Baopuxuan Tea Factory, it is based on the technique passed down in his family and after years of experiment. It is made of 147kg of arbor tea sprouts from the ancient tea garden in Luoshuidong. The cost of the sun-baked green crude tea from the arbor tea tree in that is 500 yuan per kilogram in 2007, making Pu-erh tea paste simply beyond the reach of the common people.

▲ Pu-erh tea paste

Pu-erh tea paste ▶
Pu-erh tea paste looks like charcoal. Its fragrance is similar to that of combined fragrance of brown sugar, candied dates and Pu-erh tea

◀ The tea liquid is a fragrant purplish-red. Slightly bitter at first sip, it is light and sweet thereafter, giving it a unique taste

TIPS

The Pu-erh tea paste instantly dissolves in water and leaves no sediment in the cup. The strength of the tea is easy to control. Steeping Pu-erh tea paste is special. After warming up the cup, pour boiling water into the big covered teacup (to keep the small covered teacup placed inside warm to facilitate the dissolution of the paste). Place the small covered teacup inside the big covered cup and put 2g of paste into the former. Pour boiling water. The paste will dissolve in the boiling water and the tea liquid will turn dark red. Wait a while and then stir the liquid with a teaspoon and your cup of special Pu-erh tea is ready.

(II) Crab Pincers

Crab pincers are the grass parasite on the several-hundred-year-old ancient tea trees. They are considered a type of Pu-erh tea because of their similar characterestics. Not only do they grow on the ancient Pu-erh tea trees but they are also similar to Pu-erh tea in their brewing methods. They have greater health benefits than Pu-erh tea and are more endurable. A rare and fascinating type of tea, they mostly come from the Jingmai Mountain. Today, crab pincers cost over 500 yuan/ kg.

▲ Crab pincers on ancient tea trees

▲ Dry tea: (Loose tea) looks like crab pincers, hence the name "crab pincers." This 3-year-old tea sample is brownish-red

▲ Color and taste: The liquid is light yellow, mellow with a refreshing and sweet aftertaste

▲ Brewed leaves: Brownish-red and tough, not easily broken

The sunlight-dried crab pincers are similar to raw tea in color and turn brownish-red with preservation.

(III) Old Yellow Leaves (Lao Huang Pian)

"Old yellow leaves" are the old leaves picked out in the process of producing the sun-baked green crude tea. They are preserved loose or compressed into cakes. The picked-out yellow leaves are often mistaken to be bitter and astringent.

However, a taste of the tea liquid of the boiled yellow leaves proves its mellowness and sweetness. The yellow leaves contain rich substances. In the tea-producing areas in Yunnan, the tea is a daily drink and also served to honored guests. In the current tea market, old yellow leaves occupy a special place.

The tea sample is a gift from the tea farmers in Yiwu. It is made from the yellow leaves from the arbor tea trees in Luoshuidong. The tea can be found in only a couple of shops in the market and the price is reasonable.

TIPS These are fermented old yellow leaves preserved for several years. They are reddish-brown. Their coarseness is clear from the dry sample.

Old yellow leaves from Yiwu ▲
Dry tea: Yellowish-green or reddish-brown

▲ Color and taste: The tea liquid is
orange and bright, or yellowish
green (liquid from preserved old
yellow leaves is reddish-orange),
with a mellow sweet aftertaste.
Lasting fragrance

▲ Brewed leaves: Flexible and unbroken

(IV) Old Paka (Lao Paka)

"Old paka" is a common drink in the Yunnan tea-producing areas and originally not for sale. It is made from the old leaves by heating.

The heating process for making old paka differs from making Pu-erh tea. Boil old paka in the boiling pot to destroy the activity of the enzyme in the leaves. After the leaves are withered, take them out and dry them. The dried leaves are old paka. Before making tea, it is better to roast the old paka for some time on coal fire so as to release its fragrance.

Like old yellow leaves, old paka is very popular with the local people for its special fragrance and sweet flavor. It is an indispensable daily drink in the tea-producing areas. This sample is a gift from a tea farmer in the Gaoshan Village in Yiwu. Due to the varied market demand, old paka has also appeared in the major tea markets.

TIPS Old paka must be boiled to get its special taste. As old paka is only processed in boiling water, the brewed leaves are unbroken and the redried leaves are worth collecting as samples of the ancient arbor tea tree leaves and may be used as bookmarks.

Old paka from Gaoshan Village in Yiwu ▲
Dry tea: Coarse and unbroken, light
brownish-green, prominent veins

▲ Color and taste: Tea liquid is
yellowish-green and tastes
fragrant and sweet

▲ Brewed leaves: Yellowish-green,
tough and unbroken

(V) Old Tea Lump (Lao Cha Tou)

"Old tea lump" refers to the Pu-erh tea chunk which is hard to loosen because of the temperature, humidity and stirring during pile fermentation. They are picked out by tea factories as tea lumps.

Being a lump, its outer layer has been completely fermented while its core is not. This gives the lump a unique taste—the mellow fragrance of fermented tea and the freshness of raw tea. In subsequent brews, the fresh and sweet taste of raw tea is more evident. Its flavor is far better than that of the assorted raw and processed tea or the flavored tea liquid of the two.

The tea cakes made from the lumps through compressing and the not-compressed lumps are the special "old tea lumps." The tea liquid is red as wine, smooth, fragrant and has a sweet aftertaste. It tastes good and is endurable.

This tea sample is from Menghai Tea Factory purchased from the Beijing tea market. There are many similar types of tea in the market.

TIPS Old tea lumps are compact and hard to loosen. Be careful not to hurt yourself when loosening it with a Pu-erh knife.

Old tea lumps compressed into a brick ▲
Dry tea: Same as processed tea. There are
no clear striations

▲ Color and taste: The liquid is
dark red and and tastes smooth,
fragrant and sweet

▲ Brewed leaves: Reddish-brown,
some with a dark green center due
to the incomplete fermentation
within the lump

(VI) Cereal Flower Tea (Guhuacha)

The uniqueness of "cereal flower tea" lies in its raw materials—the tea flowers blossoming at the beginning of autumn mixed with the sun-baked green crude tea leaves of the autumn tea, then compressed into cakes.

Cereal flower tea tastes like tea and smells of flowers, different from pure tea leaves. But such cereal flower tea is not sold in large quantities and is rarely seen in the market. It can mostly be seen in the tea-producing areas.

This tea sample comes from Yitian Village in Yiwu County.

TIPS Dry the flowers in the sun. They acquire a light fragrance and the strong smell of the sun. Originally, cereal flower tea referred to the tea leaves picked when the paddy rice blossomed. Today, the cereal flower tea gets its name from the tea leaves and tea flowers it is made from, and it is not a synonym of autumn tea.

Raw cereal flower tea cakes from Yiwu ▲
Dry tea: This sample is a raw cake preserved for
two years. The striations are fleshy, clear and
compact. The golden flowers are unbroken

▲ Color and taste: The liquid is bright
golden with a sweet aftertaste and
the fragrance of flowers

▲ Brewed leaves and flowers:
Unbroken leaves and flowers

Part 5

The Purchase and Preservation of Pu-erh Tea and Its Health Benefits

There are various kinds of Pu-erh tea in the market. Their prices vary greatly according to their names and raw materials. Knowing some simple ways to differentiate the various kinds of tea helps in the purchase and appreciation of the tea.

I. How to Select and Buy Pu-erh Tea

There are various kinds of tea on the market. You should have relevant knowledge and rely on your senses to choose your type of Pu-erh tea. However, the purpose of buying is of primary importance.

1. Clarify the purpose of buying Pu-erh tea

Ask yourself several questions before buying.

First, why do you want to buy Pu-erh tea? For drinking, collecting or decoration?

Most people prefer to drink processed tea, as it can be enjoyed straightaway. But it takes time to discover what works for you. Tea is a romantic drink. Tea lovers look for good taste but are likely to be cheated when buying tea. The tea may look good but may not live up to the expectations after brewing. Identifying good tea takes time and is an intrinsic part of the pleasure of tea. Right attitude is very important. Taste the tea before buying. Pay attention to the endurance of the tea and the color and taste of the tea liquid and your physical reaction after drinking it.

Collecting Pu-erh tea to make profit might not be a rational idea at all for inexperienced collectors. The selection itself involves many considerations. Besides quality, there are other considerations too, such as the available stock, market opinion, public recognition of the tea, etc.

If you want to store for drinking later, after the tea is fermented and the mellowness comes out, you need to pay attention to the raw materials and techniques affecting the fermentation of the tea.

For ornamentation, pay attention to its appearance, shape and color and historical significance.

Second, what kind of taste do you like? What is your type of Pu-erh tea?

Would you choose raw tea, processed tea, tea of tender sprouts or of old coarse leaves?

There is a big difference between raw tea and processed tea and its types. For example, tender shoots are soft and sweet, old coarse leaves are mellow, first and second batches of spring tea are less bitter than summer tea. Other differences arise from different fermentation seasons, different producers, different preservation periods or production years, etc.

Select the tea that makes you feel good. Some people have obvious adverse reactions to raw tea, such as digestive disorder, sleeplessness, excessive hunger pangs, and palpitation. Comparatively speaking, processed tea is less agitating though some may find it keeps sleep away.

Third, what is your budget?

Differences in the quality of tea result in a price range variation—ranging from less than one hundred to several thousand yuan. The single key factor distinguishing between kinds of tea is their price. From 20–30 yuan to several thousand to even several hundred thousand yuan a cake, different types of Pu-erh tea find their buyers on the market.

Decide on a price range within your budget, and then you can begin looking for the tea of your choice.

2. How to select Pu-erh tea

Selecting Pu-erh tea is no different from selecting other kinds of tea. Keep the following steps in mind:

Examine dry tea

Examining the dry tea is the first step to determine the quality of the leaves.

Tea products are graded according to the tenderness of the sun-baked green crude tea. The more tender it is, the higher it is graded. Judge the tenderness from three aspects. First, the quantity of sprouts. Tea from multiple shoots with visible tea hair is more tender. Second, the striations (i.e. how compactly are the leaves rolled). The tighter and more solid the striations, the more tender the leaves. Third, the color and shine of the leaves. The brighter and glossier, the more tender will be the leaves. High-grade loose Pu-erh tea (processed tea) appears brownish-red (or deep brown), glossy with golden hair and the striations are compact and solid.

High-grade raw Pu-erh tea cake: Dark green in color with part in dark yellow. The striations are distinct, fleshy and compact with the fragrance of green tea.

High-grade processed Pu-erh tea cake: Brownish-red. The striations are tender, fleshy and compact. Quality processed tea is fragrant. If the cake smells strange and moldy, don't buy it.

Pu-erh tea in the process of natural fermentation: The color varies from dark green to brownish-red. The striations are tender, fleshy and compact.

Examine the color of the tea liquid

The color of the tea liquid is an important index of the quality.

Color of raw tea liquid: Yellowish-green or golden.

Color of processed tea liquid: Brownish-red and bright. If the liquid is scarlet, the tea is of high quality. Dark red is the normal color, while light or dark yellow or orange is abnormal. Cloudy color indicates bad quality.

Quality processed tea has little sediment and the water is bright and red. Ordinary tea has some sediment, such as broken leaves at the bottom. But if there are too many impurities in the liquid after the tea is kept for some time, beware.

Color of naturally fermented Pu-erh tea liquid: Tea liquid colors vary according to their age. Pu-erh tea of the current year is close to that of green tea—fresh and natural. Tea fermented for 3–5 years is apricot yellow or light red whereas tea fermented for 8–10 years is red, very similar to artificially fermented tea.

Inhale the fragrance

Fragrance of processed tea: Various chemical substances reacting under the action of microbes and enzymes during post-fermentation give the tea its fragrance. Fragrance may be of date, camphorwood, longan and betel nut.

It is hard for novice tea drinkers to differentiate between mellow fragrance and moldy smell. The mellow fragrance of Pu-erh tea does not irritate the nose but is refreshing, mild and comforting, while moldy smell is irritating, impure and repellant. Similar to Tieguanyin of Oolong tea and the rock tea in Wuyi Mountain—both having their unique fragrance—the processed Pu-erh tea (including the completely fermented tea through natural fermentation) has an irresistible mellow fragrance.

Fragrance of the raw tea: Raw tea smells of the sun, honey, dates, camphorwood or simple freshness.

Fragrance of the naturally fermented Pu-erh tea: The fragrant substance in the Pu-erh tea changes during natural fermentation.

Appreciate the taste

Pu-erh tea is described as "mellow," "smooth" and with "sweet aftertaste."

Mellow is when the taste is strong, refreshing, slightly sweet, but not very fresh or irritating.

High-grade Pu-erh tea will not dry or irritate the mouth and throat. Smoothness is the indication of good pile fermentation technology and is an indispensable feature of quality Pu-erh tea.

Sweet aftertaste refers to the lingering sweetness in the mouth and the whole digestive system during or hours after its appreciation. The sweet aftertaste of Pu-erh tea is different from that of Oolong tea. Oolong tea is strong, so is its sweet aftertaste, while Pu-erh tea is mellow, and its sweet aftertaste is also mystically light, soothing and relaxing.

Taste of raw tea: Strong and irritating. The fragrance is changeable with layers. The raw tea with a sweet aftertaste is better. With high heat, the fragrance is sweet and light, and slightly astringent.

Taste of processed tea: Mild, smooth and refined. Its aftertaste is sweet and rich, and its smell mellow.

Taste of naturally fermented Pu-erh tea: Variable, depending upon the length of fermentation. The tea during fermentation has the taste of both raw tea and processed tea. Completely fermented old tea is similar in taste to processed tea, but milder and fresher.

Examine brewed leaves

To a great extent, brewed leaves reveal the secret of the raw material and the processing technique of the tea.

Brewed leaves of raw tea: Yellowish-green and bright, broken or unbroken, tough and glossy. The tea whose brewed leaves break easily when being twisted and is dark is of inferior quality.

Brewed leaves of processed tea: Dark reddish-brown. Unbroken leaves mean better quality.

Brewed leaves of naturally fermented Pu-erh tea: Unique, especially those naturally fermented leaves of the ancient wild arbor trees. The stems and veins are clear and tough.

II. How to Preserve Pu-erh Tea?

Good preservation of Pu-erh tea requires appropriate tools, clean environment, ventilation and light.

1. Environment for preserving Pu-erh tea

Tea absorbs the smell of its surroundings easily. The surroundings must be free from from strange odors. Ventilation and light are also necessary. Home-preserved Pu-erh tea should avoid being polluted by the smell of soot, cosmetics and medicine. If possible, set up a special storage room with wooden shelves.

Ventilation and light: Light and air can speed up the fermentation of tea leaves and formation of the mellow fragrance and red color of Pu-erh tea liquid. But Pu-erh tea should not be exposed to strong sunlight or stored in damp and dark environment. Open windows keeps the air fresh and helps ventilation.

Natural humidification: The tea leaves only ferment at specific temperature and humidity. The tea can be placed near some water source or a humidifier to speed up its fermentation. Such methods may be used in the northern dry areas but are not recommended.

2. Containers for preserving Pu-erh tea

Pu-erh tea can be preserved in broad bamboo leaves, clean bamboo or grass boxes, in cotton-paper packaging or other containers, but take care to:

Use containers that breathe, such as pottery and purple-clay ware. It is better to use one container to store only one kind of tea.

Avoid strange odors. Never use plastic or glass.

3. Suggestions for selecting Pu-erh tea for storing as a collector's item

Choose high-quality Pu-erh tea (raw tea). The following suggestions are for Pu-erh tea lovers to select Pu-erh tea as a collector's item:

First, choose Pu-erh tea of quality raw material. Quality raw material is the precondition for quality Pu-erh tea.

Second, choose Pu-erh tea from qualified factories for they can ensure the quality standards, equipment, technology, environment and sanitation of production. Or buy the product from standard shops.

Third, choose special Pu-erh tea, for example wild ancient arbor tea, raw tea made of old sun-baked green crude tea leaves or tender shoots or crab pincers, etc. Such special types are relatively small in quantity, from special areas and processed with special technology or of rare raw materials. They are all worthy of collection and expectation.

Fourth, choose Pu-erh tea with special memorial significance, for example memorial Pu-erh tea tailor-made for a special occasion.

4. Preservation length for Pu-erh tea

"The older, the more fragrant" is a catchphrase describing Pu-erh tea and also its most intriguing feature. But what is its maximum storage limit, 10 years or 50 years? This is difficult even for an expert to answer. Pu-erh tea (raw tea) is more valuable as it grows "older" and is better in quality with age. But like everything, it is governed by certain laws. After full maturity, the fragrance of the tea will start to deteriorate. So, "the older, the more fragrant" would not stand good. The Jingua (golden melon) tribute tea on display at the Forbidden City is about 200 years old, and its tea liquid is said to be wonderful but the flavor is not fragrant or tasty.

There is no definite time limit for the best preservation length of Pu-erh tea. Opinions vary according to the tea quality, processing techniques, preserving environment, taste of the drinker and so on. Pu-erh tea has caught the fancy of modern man merely in the last decade or so. Although there are different types of Pu-erh tea claimed to be 20, 30, or occasionally 80 years old, 80 years is still just a short period in the long history of humanity. So it is hard to calculate the optimum preservation period of Pu-erh tea as precisely as that of a French red wine. But we believe we are close to unveiling this mystery.

With Pu-erh tea, does it really matter if fermentation is perfect or not? A true tea lover need not necessarily drink only the best fermented tea, rather appreciate the various types of tea. Consider "the older, the more fragrant" to be a spiritual pursuit and longing for the special taste of Pu-erh tea.

III. Health-preserving Effect of Pu-erh Tea

Pu-erh tea in this part refers mainly to the fermented Pu-erh tea (processed tea or fermented raw tea). Pu-erh tea, though a health drink, is not a medicine. Drinking Pu-erh tea regularly may benefit the middle-aged and the elderly.

In Japan, France, Italy, South Korea, Southeast Asia and Chinese Hong Kong, Macau and Taiwan, Pu-erh tea is also called beauty tea, weight-losing tea, longevity tea, fitness tea, etc. Experiences of devoted Pu-erh tea users reveal that the tea generates warmth, reduces weight, lowers cholesterol, blood pressure and sugar, prevents arteriosclerosis, coronary heart disease and cancer. It slows down the aging process. Long-term consumption prevents cold and regulates digestion. All these benefits add to its growing popularity.

1. Drinking Pu-erh tea prevents cardiovascular problems and lowers blood pressure

The various chemical substances in Pu-erh tea can help consumers prevent the accumulation of enol and neutral fat in the blood and liver, strengthen the elasticity of the blood vessel, prevent arteriosclerosis and cerebral hemorrhage. They also strengthen the activity of the heart and blood capillaries and lower blood pressure.

Drinking Pu-erh tea improves diastole of blood vessels, slows down heart rhythm and prevents hypertension.

2. Drinking Pu-erh tea helps regulate blood fat and lose weight

Work pressure, inappropriate diet, over nutrition and lack of exercise all contribute to the accumulation of fat in our body.

Pu-erh tea suppresses the synthesis of liver cholesterol and effectively lowers the amount of cholesterol, triglyceride and free fatty acid in the blood. It also increases the discharge rate of cholesterol and dampens the oxidization of low-density fat protein.

3. Drinking Pu-erh tea regulates digestion and alleviates constipation

Fermented Pu-erh tea is mild and as long as its strength is suitable, it will not irritate the digestive system but improve it by increasing the secretion of gastric juice, promoting digestion and alleviating constipation.

4. Drinking Pu-erh tea can help prevent cancer and resist radiation

The anticancer organic substances in tea include tea phenol, theophylline and various vitamins. The anticancer inorganic substances mainly are zinc, molybdenum, manganese, etc. Experiments show that tea phenol has stronger effect in resisting oxidation and radiation than Vitamin E.

Among all types of tea, Yunnan Pu-erh tea can best prevent cancer and resist radiation. As a first-grade tea-producing area in China, Yunnan boasts excellent soil, temperate climate, rich rainfall, all of which are especially conducive to tea trees.

5. Drinking Pu-erh tea slows down aging

The antiaging effect of Pu-erh tea comes from the tannic acid in its leaves, which is 18 times more effective than Vitamin E. The tea phenol can disrupt the activity of the free radicals in the human body and the catechin is effective in resisting oxidization and aging. The big-leaf tea from Yunnan contains more catechin than other types of tea, making its antiaging effect greater than other kinds of tea. Moreover, during the processing of Pu-erh tea, its macromolecular polysaccharose substances are converted into a large quantity of dissoluble monosaccharide, and its Vitamin C doubles in quantity. Such substances play important roles in strengthening the immune system and facilitating health preservation, body building and extending life.

6. Pu-erh tea can improve looks

Once known as "tea for the elderly," Pu-erh tea is today the "tea for women." The reason is that it regulates metabolism, speeds up blood circulation and regulates and balances the body functions. It enhances physical beauty.

7. Pu-erh tea can effectively promote blood circulation

The sensation of feeling the cold comes from bad blood circulation and is a common symptom among women. Pu-erh tea effectively promotes blood circulation and warms the body. Adding ginger will improve the effect.

8. Pu-erh tea diminishes inflammation, suppresses bacteria and protects teeth

There are many active physiological substances in Pu-erh tea which have obvious bacteriostasis. Research in the pharmaceutical industry and clinical experiments show that Pu-erh tea can resist bacteria. This is because of the rich tea phenol in the big-leaf tea of Yunnan. Tea trees absorb fluorine from the soil, so tea is rich in fluorine, which is effective in protecting and strengthening teeth. Besides, the tea phenol chemical compound, protect the teeth from caries and get rid of bad breath.

Mr. Yang Rudai (right) and I

Acknowledgments

I am deeply indebted to Mr. Yang Rudai and other tea producers and experts of the older generation. The writing and publishing of this book is due to their support and help.

I have learned a lot from the Pu-erh tea expert Mr. Zeng Yunrong, and thank my tea farmer and producer friends who have been growing and producing tea for generations.

Thank you Mr. Wang Jiliang and Ms. Fu Jie, Ms. Yao Xueyuan and Ms. Men Xuefengfor your contribution to this work. My gratitude also goes to the experts and scholars whose works have been referred to.

Wang Jidong

A Blang woman tea maker in Jingmai Mountain

Four generations of inheritors of the ancient Baopuxuan tea factory in the ancient township in Yiwu

▲ Pu-erh tea expert Mr. Zeng Yunrong, nicknamed "the Old Tea Tree," who devoted his life to growing tea in the tea-producing area, caring for the tender shoots like his grandchildren

▲ Caravan captain of the Yi ethnic group and his folks

▲ Versatile Yi tea farmers

▲ A Hani household in Ning'er County who live by growing tea